PROFESSIONAL ISSUES FOR SOCIAL WORKERS IN SCHOOLS

PAPERS FROM THE
2nd NASW NATIONAL CONFERENCE
ON SCHOOL SOCIAL WORK
MAY 7-9, 1981, WASHINGTON, D.C.

NATIONAL ASSOCIATION
OF SOCIAL WORKERS
SILVER SPRING, MD

371.2022
P 964

International Standard Book No.: 0-87101-095-X

Library of Congress Catalog Card No.: 81-86368

NASW Catalog No.: CPB-095-C

Printed in the U.S.A.

CONTRIBUTORS

(Positions are those held at the time of the conference, May 1981)

JOHN ALDERSON, MSW, Professor, School of Social Work, Florida State University, Tallahassee.

NANCY KRAMER BANCHY, MSW, School Social Work Specialist, Minnesota Department of Education, St. Paul.

JULIE COOLIDGE, Ed.S., Director of Special Education, T-O-W Special Education Coop, Wadena Public Schools, Wadena, Minnesota.

LYNN CORBIN, MSW, School Social Worker, Board of Cooperative Educational Services, Rensselaer/Columbia/Greene Counties, Castleton, New York.

C. RICHARD DONAHUE, MSW, School Social Worker, Board of Cooperative Educational Services, Putnam/Northern Westchester Education Center, Yorktown Heights, New York.

ROBERT J. GALLAGHER, School Social Worker, Area Education Agency #1, Dubuque, Iowa.

CLAIRE B. GALLANT, MSW, Consultant and Trainer, National Association of Social Workers, Washington, D.C.

HARRIS GOLDSTEIN, DSW, Professor, School of Social Work, Florida State University, Tallahassee.

JOAN Y. SEMBLY HARRIS, MA, Educational Specialist, School Social Work Service, Office of Social and Psychological Services, Baltimore City Public Schools, Baltimore, Maryland.

MABLE T. EMANUEL HAWKINS, Ph.D., Associate Professor, School of Social Work, University of Pittsburgh, Pittsburgh, Pennsylvania.

SALLY NORTH HOOPER, MSW, Clinical Social Worker, People Care, Natick, Massachusetts.

ALICE E. LAMONT, Ph.D., Associate Professor, School of Social Work, Wayne State University, Detroit, Michigan.

E. VIRGINIA LAPHAM, M.Ed., MSW, Research Associate, University of Maryland, Baltimore.

LORETTA LOPEZ, MSW, Social Work Specialist, Albuquerque Public Schools, Albuquerque, New Mexico.

WALLACE LORNELL, MSW, School Social Worker, Division of Pupil Personnel Services, New York State Education Department, Albany.

RAY H. MacNAIR, Ph.D., Assistant Professor, School of Social Work, University of Georgia, Athens.

ELIZABETH L. McKINNEY, MSW, Assistant Professor, School of Social Work, University of Georgia, Athens.

MARJORIE McQUEEN MONKMAN, DSW, Associate Professor, School of Social Work, University of Illinois, Urbana.

STEVE L. MONTOYA, MSW, School Social Worker, District Diagnostic Center, Special Education, Albuquerque, New Mexico.

CHRIS ANLAUF SABATINO, MSW, doctoral candidate, National Catholic School of Social Service, The Catholic University of America, Washington, D.C.

RODNEY G. SCHOFIELD, Ed.D., Supervisor, Social Work Services, Colorado Springs Public Schools, Colorado Springs, Colorado.

ELIZABETH M. TIMBERLAKE, DSW, Associate Professor, National Catholic School of Social Service, The Catholic University of America, Washington, D.C.

BETTY L. WELSH, MSW, Professor, School of Social Work, Wayne State University, Detroit, Michigan.

TERRY ZIELINSKI, MSW, School Social Worker, T-O-W Special Education Coop, Wadena Public Schools, Wadena, Minnesota.

KAREN ZIMMERMAN, BSW, graduate student, School of Social Work, Florida State University, Tallahassee.

CONTENTS

PREFACE

The papers that constitute this volume were presented under the auspices of the National Association of Social Workers (NASW) at the association's Second National Conference on School Social Work on May 8, 1981, in Washington, D.C. The presentations were made in the section of the program entitled Professional Issues Affecting Social Work Practice in the Schools. The issues addressed in these forums had been discussed during meetings of the NASW Practice Advancement Council on Social Work Services in Schools. In developing the conference program, the NASW Conference Planning Task Force, in collaboration with the council, designated this particular segment of the conference for inclusion in a published proceedings.

The ideas addressed in these papers have an important professional impact on social work practice in the schools, and although the work of the authors is entirely their own, in several cases they did work directly with the council. For example, Alderson, Goldstein, and Zimmerman's study of the practice implications of P.L. 94-142 was initiated at the request of the council when Alderson was a member of that group. Also related to P.L. 94-142 is Timberlake, Sabatino, and Hooper's article on the future of school social work practice.

Gallagher's work on the comprehensive assessment of handicapped children was reviewed by his colleagues on the Practice Advancement Council during his term of office with that committee. Gallant's article on marketable social work skills derives from her work as a consultant-trainer under an Office of Special Education grant secured by NASW to train school social workers and other special education personnel to act as mediators under P.L. 94-142.

Through her work as a consultant on a grant sponsored by the NASW Practice Advancement Council, Lapham consulted on the issue of state certification with school social workers in six states throughout the country. Supporting and expanding her overview are articles describing issues related to certification in three specific states: Montoya and Lopez examine certification efforts in New Mexico, Harris presents perspectives in relation to the Maryland State Department of Education, and Banchy discusses attempts to upgrade standards in Minnesota.

The other issues dealt with in this volume have also been on the council's agenda. These issues include the education of social workers for practice in schools, which is treated from three approaches in articles by Hawkins, by Lamont and Welsh, and by Corbin, Donahue, and Lornell.

McKinney and MacNair explore the problem of bias in the development of the social assessment, and in a related article, Schofield describes the use of self-concept measures in assessment of student functioning as well as the evaluation of program effectiveness. Varied approaches to school social work are examined by Zielinski and Coolidge, who discuss barriers to the implementation of a systems model of practice, and by Monkman, who presents a model for differential levels of practice.

The members of the Practice Advancement Council and of the Conference Planning Task Force join in hoping that this collection of papers will be of value to social workers with a particular interest in the relationship of their profession to the education setting.

LORRAINE DAVIS
Chairperson, Practice Advancement Council
on Social Work Service in Schools

ANNE MITCHELL
Chairperson, Planning Task Force,
Second NASW National Conference
on School Social Work

THE IMPACT OF P. L. 94-142 ON
SCHOOL SOCIAL WORK PRACTICE

JOHN ALDERSON, HARRIS GOLDSTEIN,
AND KAREN ZIMMERMAN

This article reports on some of the impacts on school social work practice of P.L. 94-142--The Education for All Handicapped Children Act of 1975. The study was originated and sponsored during 1979-80 by the Provisional Council on Social Work Services in the Schools of the National Association of Social Workers (NASW). The data were analyzed by the School of Social Work, Florida State University. It was expected that information derived from the study would help NASW to purposefully influence the implementation of the law, and would be useful to school social workers.

The overall objective of this study was to determine whether and in what ways the advent of P.L. 94-142 has impacted on and changed various selected dimensions of school social work practice. The specific questions which this study attempted to answer are as follows:

● How much time do school social workers spend in implementing P.L. 94-142? How has this changed over the past several years?

● How satisfied are school social workers with the amount of time they devote to implementing P.L. 94-142?

● Are school social work services commonly accepted and utilized as part of the Individualized Educational Programs (IEPs)? 1/

● What school social work services are most commonly included in the IEP? What are the least utilized services?

● What are the most and the least frequent functions performed by school social workers in the implementation of the provisions of P.L. 94-142?

● What are the major problems and concerns of school social workers as related to P.L. 94-142?

● What proportion of their time do school social workers spend in carrying out the four stated functions under the related services provisions of the law?

● To what extent are school systems working out interagency agreements, and how active have school social workers been directly working on these agreements? 2/

● What practice model, as derived from ratings of goal importance, is the predominant model used by school social work respondents? How does this compare with previous studies of tasks in school social work, and other literature descriptions of practice models? Has the advent of P.L. 94-142 altered the practice models utilized by school social workers?

LITERATURE REVIEW

The marked increase in recent years of professional literature related to P.L. 94-142 is an evidence of the far-reaching effects of this legislation. 3/ Social work literature during the first year after passage of the law was virtually nonexistent. Professional recognition of the need and importance for social work role clarification began in 1977, when leaders in the field of school social work gathered in Athens, Georgia, for a workshop on this law. The conference proceedings, published by NASW, helped to disseminate a more clarified role, thereby assisting school social workers in their approaches to the legislation. The proceedings included eight articles on a variety of issues pertaining to the school social worker's role and skills related to meeting requirements of this legislation. 4/

During 1978, more articles appeared in the school social work journals. NASW published Federal Legislation and the School Social Worker, edited by Evertts. This book contained eight articles regarding the major legislation affecting school social workers and the role they could take in implementation. 5/ Problems related to the law, and possible negative implications were identified by some authors in other publications. Weatherley discussed various problems, including routinization of assessment and educational planning, insufficient funding, and the tendency to meet only minimum requirements rather than maximum amount. 6/ Brull cited numerous problems which could be associated with the legislation and its implementation. 7/

Both the amount and scope of the literature concerning P.L. 94-142 increased dramatically during 1979. In the three main school social work journals, Social Work in Education, School Social Work Journal, and School Social Work Quarterly, there were at least nine articles that dealt directly with P.L. 94-142 and/or its implications and practice. Indications were that the role and function of school social workers were broadening as they implemented the law and provided "related services." Creative service delivery techniques and practice models were suggested for providing services the law mandated. One function of the role expansion included accountability. Constable expressed the opinion that school social workers were at a "crucial junction" in 1979 and could define their own destiny. He defined aspects of accountability and envisioned an expansion of the school social worker's role to include coordination of services and interagency agreements. 8/ Ensuring student and parental rights was another social work responsibility discussed by Jankovic. She stressed the need to have a working knowledge of the law to provide due process services regarding discipline, basic children's rights, confidentiality, and policymaking. She reemphasized the roles of advocate, mediator, clarifier, arbitrator, plaintiff, and defendant. 9/

In other articles, specific service delivery techniques were expounded by Treger for psychosocial assessments; by Gallant for mediation; by Hodgman and Vogel for in-service to children about handicapping conditions; and Welsh for an evaluation and accountability model. 10/

Thus far, one published account has appeared on research related to school social work and P.L. 94-142. Timberlake, Sabatino, and Hooper studied the informational inputs made by each member of the interdisciplinary assessment team. This helped them discover the variables which played a part in group decisions about educational planning for the handicapped. The findings supported a multidisciplinary approach to service delivery issues raised by the legislation. 11/

Method. A twenty-four-item questionnaire, ten of which pertained to to demographic information, was designed for the purpose of obtaining answers to the questions listed above. The sample was drawn from the October 1980 mailing list comprising 7,714 names utilized by NASW in distributing the School Social Work Bulletin. This listing is commonly used as a basis for indicating the number of NASW-affiliated school social workers in the United States. It is also used to inform membership and to seek responsive action about matters of concern to school social work. Approximately 964 questionnaires, one of every eight names on NASW's roster, were sent from the national NASW office during November 1980. Completed questionnaires were returned to the School of Social Work, Florida State University, for analysis.

Description of Respondents. Two hundred and thirteen usable returns were received, representing 22 percent of the 964 questionnaires sent out. No follow-up request for returns was made. The respondents were predominantly white (84 percent) and female (64 percent). Only 4 percent of the respondents were black, with 5 percent Asian-American, and 3 percent Chicano-Mexican American. The largest age grouping was between 30 and 39 years (38 percent), with the second largest 50 and over (30 percent). Almost one in five (19 percent) were between 40 and 49 years of age. Over eight in ten respondents (85 percent) held a master's as their highest degree with seven in ten (73 percent) possessing the MSW degree. About 7 percent held either the BSW or other bachelor's degrees. Approximately one in ten (12 percent) held other kinds of master's degrees.

Eight out of ten (85 percent) held the title "school social worker." Approximately four in ten (40 percent) reported assignment to four or more separate schools, and a similar proportion (40 percent) were assigned to one, two, or three separate schools. Two-thirds of the respondents (66 percent) were assigned to elementary schools, with almost half reporting assignments in intermediate and secondary schools, providing evidence that many respondents serve all three levels. Close to one-half (45 percent) worked in school systems with a school population between 3,000 and 24,999. There were 17 percent each in the two categories of less than 3,000 and between 24,999 and 100,000.

Almost half (48 percent) had extensive experience as school social workers, having worked in this capacity for over one-half of their time between six and fifteen years. One in three (34 percent) had worked five years or less, and one in ten (11 percent) for sixteen years and over. Replies were received from twenty-eight states. No effort was made to analyze these on a regional or a state-by-state basis. Despite a lower rate of returns, these data appear to be essentially similar to demographic data from the NASW study of 1976 and the Meares study of 1977. 12/

FINDINGS

Initiation of Services. During school years 1977-1978 and 1978-1979, marked increases in initiating services related to P.L. 94-142 were reported by respondents. The peak year in which respondents began working to implement tasks related to P.L. 94-142 was school year 1978-1979; three in ten reported initiating services that year. A gradual buildup occurred from 1975 to 1978. The crest for initiation of services evidently was reached in 1978-1979 as only one in ten reported started services in the 1979-1980 school year. One in three estimated the percentage of time devoted to those tasks the year they began was 0-20 percent. About one in two reported spending 40 percent or less of their time the first year.

Time Devoted to P.L. 94-142. An upsurge in professional time and energy occurred during 1980 and 1981 among the school social worker respondents in relation to implementing P.L. 94-142. For school year 1980-1981, approximately one in three respondents reported spending from 81 to 100 percent of their time in fulfilling tasks related to the law, while the remaining respondents reported time allocations in roughly equal amounts in the various time blocks from 0 to 20 percent to 61 to 80 percent. In contrast, for school year 1978-1979, just two years earlier, slightly above one in five reported spending 81 to 100 percent of their time, while just under one in five reported spending 41 to 60 percent of their time.

Satisfaction-Dissatisfaction. Slightly over one-half (56 percent) of the respondents reported satisfaction with the amount of time they spent on tasks related to P.L. 94-142. However, one in four expressed dissatisfaction and would prefer spending less time on these tasks. A smaller proportion (15 percent) also expressed dissatisfaction, but wanted more time allocated to the tasks related to the law.

Implementing Individualized Educational Plans. Almost nine out of ten (87 percent) reported a general acceptance of school social work services as one of the options in implementing IEPs. The respondents performed a wide range of functions related to implementing IEPs. All thirteen listed

4

school social work services were utilized at some time as one of the IEP services (only 8 percent reported that "other" services were offered). 13/ Two of the three most frequently performed tasks related to implementing the IEP were clinical in nature. However, frequently performed functions also included consultation, liaison between home and school, and coordination of services, all of which have been identified as highly relevant functions of the school social worker.

Services performed by 75 percent or more of the respondents were, in rank order:

1. Consultation to the teacher (87 percent).
2. Consultation to the parent (85 percent).
3. Liaison between home and school (84 percent).
4. Coordination of services with community (81 percent).
5. Casework counseling for the parents (76 percent).

When respondents were asked to specify from the listing of services the three most frequently performed social work services, they replied as follows (the listings in the following groups of rankings may total more than the number of respondents because of the way the question was worded):

1. Casework counseling to the child (126 listings).
2. Consultation with the teacher (94 listings).
3. Casework counseling to the parent (70 listings).

The fourth- and fifth-ranked most frequently performed services were:

4. Liaison role between home and school (60 listings).
5. Coordination and service integration with community resources (56 listings).

The three social work services reported as least frequently performed were:

1. Mediation between the parent and school system (99 listings).
2. Family group counseling (64 listings).
3. Direct classroom intervention (64 listings).

GOAL IMPORTANCE AND TIME ALLOCATION

The goal which has been primarily identified as traditional-clinical in focus was selected as the paramount goal of the respondents. The goal of implementing P.L. 94-142 was one of the three higher ranked goals; it is unlikely that this would have appeared as a major goal if this study had been conducted several years earlier. The low-ranked goals are primarily those which relate to school-community-pupil relations, community conditions, and development of programs for students affected by poverty and other disadvantages.

The item related to goal importance and time expenditure for each goal was composed of six statements derived from descriptions in the literature of five major practice models, plus one statement related to the goal of implementing P.L. 94-142. The goal statements are listed below, with the practice model identified in parentheses. 14/

1. To enable the pupil identified as having a school related social-emotional difficulty to function more effectively (Traditional-Clinical Model).
2. To alter school norms and conditions which are dysfunctional for students (School Change Model).
3. To develop community understanding and support of school. (Community-School Model).
4. To develop programs for students affected by poverty and/or other disadvantaged conditions (School-Community-Pupil Model). (The definition of this model contains two separate statements. See Item 6 for the second part of the definition.)
5. To facilitate communication, interaction, and mutual support among all members of the school system (i.e., parents, students, staff, community). (School Change Model.)
6. To help target groups of students to more effectively use learning opportunities by bringing about changes in the system of school-community-pupil relations. (School-Community-Pupil Model.)
7. To participate in activities designed to ensure full education for all handicapped students, as specified in P.L. 94-142.

The three top-ranked goals, in order of selection, were:

1. To enable the pupil identified as having a school related social-emotional difficulty to function more effectively (rated very important by 84 percent).
2. To facilitate communications, interaction, and mutual support among all members of the school system (i.e. parents, students, staff, community). (Rated very important by 70 percent.)
3. To participate in activities designed to ensure full education for all handicapped students, as specified in P.L. 94-142 (56 percent rated very important).

There appears to be a fairly close matching between the goal ranked as most important and the time allocated to achieve it. For the top-ranked goal, over four in ten (45 percent) spent a great deal of time (twenty hours or more per week) and three in ten (30 percent) spent from six to nineteen hours per week in tasks intended to assist the child having a school related socioemotional difficulty. A level of frustration may be evident in the item related to the second-ranked goal, in that seven in ten rated this as very important, while only one in four was able to spend twenty or more hours per week on this task; fully two-thirds (68 percent) spent only a slight (one to five hours) or a moderate amount of time (six to nineteen hours) per week. In the item related to implementation of P.L. 94-142, some respondents are probably dissatisfied as almost six in ten rated this as

6

very important and only three in ten spent twenty or more hours on such tasks.

The three lower-ranked goals related to importance were:

1. To develop programs for students affected by poverty and/or other disadvantaged conditions (30 percent for each slightly, moderately, and very important).
2. To help target groups of students to more effectively use learning opportunities by bringing about changes in the system of school-community-pupil relations (24 percent rated of slight importance, 36 percent rated moderately important, and 25 percent very important).
3. To develop community understanding and support of school (24 percent rated slightly, 33 percent rated moderately, and 30 percent rated very important).

The time expenditures for all three lower ranked goals appeared to relate closely to time expenditures. Approximately eight in ten of the respondents spent only five hours or less per week on tasks related to these goals.

The middle-ranked goal of the seven was "To alter school norms and conditions which are dysfunctional for students" (19 percent rated slightly, 31 percent moderately, and 45 percent very important). Evidence of frustration appears in that over four in ten rated this as very important, but fully six in ten (60 percent) spend only one to five hours and three in twenty (14 percent) did not spend any of their time on tasks related to this goal.

FUNCTIONS PERFORMED

Respondents carried out a wide range of functions related to the implementation of P.L. 94-142. All seventeen listed functions were utilized by the workers as part of implementing P.L. 94-142. 15/ In general, there is congruence between the functions identified as most frequently utilized, and the importance assigned by the workers to these tasks. The four functions most frequently performed are also designated as very important by two out of three respondents. This finding appears to be supportive of the earlier finding that the model of practice generally identified as traditional-clinical is the predominant model used by respondents in this study. Writing reports is a frequently performed function, but is not considered of high importance by most respondents.

Seven functions were reported by 70 percent or more of the respondents as being performed to implement P.L. 94-142: These were:

1. Consultation with parents (84 percent perform; 75 percent rated as very important; 13 percent moderately important).
2. Consultation with teachers and other school personnel (84 percent perform; 65 percent rated very important; 21 percent moderate).
3. Liaison between home and school (81 percent perform; 64 percent rated very important; 19 percent moderate).

4. Psychosocial study and assessment of children who may be handicapped (81 percent perform; 70 percent rated very important; 15 percent moderate).

5. Writing reports (77 percent perform; 29 percent rated very important; 32 percent moderate).

6. Participation in planning for the IEP (73 percent perform; 36 percent rated very important; 32 percent moderate importance).

7. Participation in the process of locating children who may be handicapped (70 percent perform; 43 percent rated very important, 22 percent moderate importance).

When respondents were requested to specify from the listing the four functions they most frequently perform, the results were:

1. Psychosocial study and assessment of children who may be handicapped (157 listed; 70 percent rated as very important).

2. Consultation with parents (115 listed; 76 percent rated as very important).

3. Consultation with teachers and other school personnel (101 listed; 65 percent rated as very important).

4. Liaison between home and school (98 listed; 64 percent rated as very important).

The six least frequently reported functions were as follows. (The ratings on importance are not listed here due to the fact that only about one-half of the respondents listed the importance of these low-ranked functions. This low response may well be a sign of low importance placed on these activities. Also, when a function was not performed, there was a tendency not to rate its importance, even though this was requested.)

1. Due process mediation (26 percent performed).
2. Leadership and policymaking activities (29 percent performed).
3. Preschool screening (36 percent performed).
4. Implementation of due process provisions of P.L. 94-142 (38 percent performed).
5. Leadership role in in-service training (43 percent performed).
6. Evaluation of achievement of objectives (44 percent performed).

The request that respondents list the four least frequently performed functions actually yielded five, due to a virtual tie for fourth and fifth place. These were:

1. Implementation of the IEP (84 listed; 34 percent rated very important, 29 percent important).

2. Periodic reviews (66 listed; 21 percent very important; 19 percent important).

3. Leadership role in in-service education and training (66 listed; 16 percent very important; 29 percent important).

4. Locating children who may be handicapped (63 listed; 43 percent very important; 22 percent important).

5. Preschool screening (62 listed; 15 percent very important; 17 percent important).

The functions of "coordination and service integration within the school district" and "promoting the coordination and integration of school services with community based services," were ranked seventh (fifty-four listings) and ninth (fifty-two listings) respectively among least frequently performed functions.

Special comment will be made on the two items related to the IEP since gathering information on this aspect was a goal of the study. The data on this item showed that 73 percent of respondents participated in planning for the IEP and that 36 percent rated it very important and 32 percent rated it moderately important. Concerning implementation of the IEP, 62 percent performed; 34 percent rated it very important; and 29 percent rated it moderately important. (While all 213 respondents responded as to whether this function was performed, only 157 rated the importance of this task.) The ratings on importance were similar for the function of participation in planning for the IEP, which was one of the frequently performed functions. It would appear that most of the respondents have opportunities for inputs into planning of the IEPs, six in ten are involved in implementation, but neither of these activities is considered of utmost importance by most of the respondents.

PROBLEMS RELATED TO P.L. 94-142

Lack of personnel is the most severe problem identified, with insufficient numbers of social workers and student services personnel available to carry out provisions of the law. This in all likelihood relates to a major concern about inadequate funding. Serious concern is evident about excessive time required for completion of forms, reports, various paperwork--what is often called "red tape." Respondents are strongly concerned that the requirements of the law are draining school social work resources away from children needing help through regular education, that needed services are often unavailable at no cost to the parent, and that students are increasingly being labeled. There is little concern over social assessments, as related to time required, completion of these for each eligible child, or their being performed by persons other than school social workers.

Respondents were requested to rate fourteen problems and/or concerns related to P.L. 94-142 on a four-point scale of seriousness, from "Of No Concern" through "Extremely Severe." 16/ The results are depicted below:

Extremely Severe

1. Not enough social workers (52 percent rated Extremely Severe).
2. Inadequate funding (44 percent rated Extremely Severe).
3. Not enough student services personnel (39 percent rated Extremely Severe).
4. Too much time on forms, reports, paperwork ("red tape") (67 percent).

Combined Ratings--Moderate and Extremely Severe

9

1. Not enough social workers (76 percent).
2. Inadequate funding (69 percent).
3. Too much time on forms, reports, paperwork ("red tape") (67 percent).
4. Draining of school social work resources away from children needing help through regular education (66 percent).
5. Not enough student services personnel (65 percent).
6. Needed medical, mental health, and social services are often unavailable at "no cost" to the parent (61 percent).
7. Increased labeling of students (50 percent).

Combined Ratings - Of No Concern and Of Marginal Concern

1. Excessive pressure to mainstream (77 percent).
2. Too much time spent on due process provisions (71 percent).
3. Social assessments by personnel other than school social workers (71 percent).

Of No Concern

1. Social assessments are performed by personnel other than school social workers (53 percent rated Of No Concern).
2. Too much time on psychosocial assessments (38 percent rated Of No Concern).
3. Social assessments are not prepared for each child considered for or enrolled in special education (38 percent rated Of No Concern).

RELATED SERVICES AND INTERAGENCY AGREEMENTS

One item asked the school social work respondents to estimate from the time actually assigned to work on P.L. 94-142 and the percentage of time spent in fulfilling the four services specified as part of related services in P.L. 94-142. The services are: (1) preparing a social or developmental history on a handicapped child, (2) group and individual counseling with the child and family, (3) working with those problems in a child's living situation (home, school, and community) that affect the child's adjustment in school, and (4) mobilizing school and community resource to enable the child to receive maximum benefit from his or her educational program.

The data showed a fairly equal distribution over the first three services specified, ranging from four to five out of ten respondents spending less than one-fourth of their time in preparing social or developmental histories, in group or individual counseling, and in working with problems in a child's living situation (home, school, and community) that affect the child's adjustment in school. The least frequently performed grouping of services, with about seven in ten reporting spending less than one-fourth of their time, was that of mobilizing school and community resources for the maximum benefit of the child in his or her educational program.

Only a small proportion (two in ten) of the school social work respondents are implementing interagency agreements, even though a majority (six in ten) of the school systems in which they work have developed such agreements. In school systems which had developed interagency agreements, close to two-thirds reported that one to three agency agreements had been developed, and approximately 20 percent reported four to six agency agreements. Of the twenty-eight respondents who indicated how many interagency agreements they had been active in developing, twenty-three indicated they had worked on between one and three agreements.

IMPLICATIONS AND CONCLUSIONS

An overriding conclusion is that school social workers have moved vigorously in recent years toward meeting the challenges and far-reaching mandates of the Education for All Handicapped Children Act. Most of the respondents in this study were satisfied with the amount of time devoted to implementing the law, but a sizable group (one in four) expressed dissatisfaction and desired less time to work on tasks related to P.L. 94-142. This latter finding may be associated with the serious concern of the respondents that the mandates of the law, combined with inadequate funding and insufficient personnel, drain resources away from children in regular education.

The study appears to refute concerns expressed about social assessments. Respondents did not view as problems the time required to complete the assessments, that some children are not receiving assessments, or that personnel other than school social workers are performing these services. Possibly the data could be subject to another interpretation, namely, that the respondents have little regard for the importance of these assessments, do not care whether each eligible child receives one, and do not care who performs them. However, a more plausible interpretation, and one related to the intent in formulating these items, is that the respondents view eligible children as generally receiving proper and adequate social assessments and that professional school social workers are performing these services.

Based on this study, school social work services are well accepted as one of the options in implementing IEPs, and a majority (six in ten) of respondents were involved in carrying out IEPs. While these findings may offer some reassurance to those who fear that the school social worker's role might be limited primarily to assessments, there is a troubling note. Implementing the IEP emerged as the least frequently utilized service. This may indicate that the services of school social workers are not being fully utilized in IEPs. This could relate to the finding that funds and personnel are insufficient, and that the workers may be pressed into performing other mandated functions. This latter finding would support the NASW position paper to the Bureau of Education for the Handicapped (BEH), that related services necessary to each handicapped child's educational program must be provided by qualified personnel. 17/ The respondents viewed psychosocial study and assessments as a much more important function than that of planning or implementing the IEP. Thus, low involvement in IEP implementation could partly be a matter of the workers' own preferences as to what functions should be carried out.

Based on the analysis of goals and goal importance, the major practice approach appears to be, with some exceptions, that of the traditional-clinical model. 18/ The second-ranked goal of respondents related to the definition of the social interaction model, which is not clinically oriented, and is based on an ecological orientation related to the mutual need of persons and systems for one another and their reciprocal influences on one another. 19/ Unfortunately, despite its high ratings, little time was spent by most workers in carrying out this goal. Low-ranked goals were those defining the community-school model, and the school-change model, lending further weight to the conclusion that a clinically oriented model is the major practice orientation.

Conclusions as to practice models related specifically to P.L. 94-142 must be based on items related to functions performed by respondents which pertain to this legislation. Three of the seven most frequently performed functions related to the IEP and overall implementation of P.L. 94-142 were clinical in nature (others related to consultation with parents and school, and liaison activities). Lower-ranked functions included leadership activities related to policymaking and in-service training, and direct classroom intervention. Thus, the practice picture would seem to be strongly skewed in favor of services primarily oriented toward the individual child, with comparatively small amounts of effort devoted to interventions likely to impact on the school as a system, and to affect larger groups of students.

Thus, a crucial question raised by this study relates to the proper balance between micro and macro interventions. Are school social workers assigned to implementing P.L. 94-142 fully using their interventive skills with school and community systems for the benefit of students? The data suggest that they are not. Lower-ranked goals, and infrequently performed functions tended to be those related to school and community interventions. Specifically, these include such roles as leadership in policymaking and in-service training activities, and coordination of school and community resources.

A major conclusion of the study reported on in this paper is that the practice stance appears to be predominantly clinical in orientation. This finding seems to be more congruent with the Costin study of more than a decade ago. The question of appropriate and viable practice models for implementing social work tasks related to P.L. 94-142 has received some recent attention in the literature. Timberlake, Sabatino, and Hooper seemed to question the necessity of searching out a specific model for school social work practice and P.L. 94-142, stating in part that

> the data collected in this study did not have to be given
> a label such as the "clinical-casework approach" or "home-
> school-community" approach. Rather, the data shows that
> the many school social work practice tasks which form an
> ecosystem framework can be used to describe what a school
> social worker does. And, even when a Federal law man-
> dates changes in that social work setting, there is
> not a major trauma for the school social work practitioner

since the ecosystem framework, by its very nature, accommodates such an event. 20/

Meares stressed the advantage of a systems model as a practice approach to implementing P.L. 94-142. 21/ She maintains that the systems model is not in conflict with traditional treatment approaches. It provides a broad and comprehensive framework for viewing a complex organization, and also calls for identifying a unit of interventions, whether it be individual, group, organization, or community focused. She stresses that both the micro and the macro levels of intervention are equally important for effective services delivery. Much professional attention has been focused recently on "burnout" in the helping professions. It requires but little "reading between the lines" of this study to sense that the social work respondents, while not necessarily becoming burned out, are in a stressful situation in relation to the mandates of this legislation and the carrying out of professional services of high quality. The concerns about inadequate funding, insufficient manpower, frustration at being unable to carry out highly rated functions, excessive paperwork, labeling, being pulled away from services to the total school population, all combine to form a highly stressful package.

These problems taken together may signal a serious threat to school social work as it has been known and as it has been developing in recent years. If the problems cited are not resolved and continue there is the possibility that erosion will occur in important aspects of the school social worker's role as related to meeting the needs of target groups of children, offering services to children in regular school programs, addressing the ecological system of the school, serving as an advocate for policy changes which affect all students, and other efforts geared toward all children in schools.

It would appear that further study would be useful as to the effects of P.L. 94-142 on school social work practice. Certainly NASW, school social workers, other school personnel, and parents need to work vigorously to alleviate the major twin problems of inadequate funding and insufficient staffing. Shifts in the practice role of school social workers more toward school and community interventions will in all likelihood be highly difficult unless these underlying problems are resolved.

NOTES AND REFERENCES

1. "Bureau's Draft Policy on IEPs Leaves Service Provision Gaps," NASW School Social Work Bulletin, March 1980, p. 1.

2. "Inadequate Funds, Services Clashes, Plague P.L. 94-142," ibid., p. 3.

3. A thorough, but not exhaustive review of the professional literature, mainly in the school social work area, located seventy-six professional articles and books related to P.L. 94-142.

4. Richard J. Anderson, Molly Freeman, and Richard L. Edwards, eds., School Social Work and P.L. 94-142: The Education for All Handicapped Children Act (Washington, D.C.: National Association of Social Workers, 1977).

5. Jeanne Evertts, ed., Federal Legislation and the School Social Worker (Washington, D.C.: National Association of Social Workers, 1978).

6. Richard Weatherley, "PL 94-142: Social Work's Role in Local Implementation," in Anderson, Freeman, and Edwards, op. cit., pp. 9-13.

7. H. Frank Brull, "PL 94-142: Boon or Bust," School Social Work Journal, 3 (Fall 1978), pp. 31-36.

8. Robert Constable, "Toward the Construction of Role in an Emergent Social Work Specialization," School Social Work Quarterly, 1 (Summer 1979), pp. 139-148.

9. Joanne Jankovic, "Law and School Social Work," Social Work in Education, 2 (October 1979), pp. 5-17.

10. Lynda Treger, "A Model for Psychosocial Assessment," School Social Work Quarterly, 1 (Fall 1979), pp. 209-218; Claire B. Gallant, "New Use of Skills for PL 94-142," Social Work in Education, 1 (October 1978); N. Hodgman and P. Vogel, "Needed: In-Service for Children," School Social Work Journal, 3 (Spring 1979), pp. 93-94; and Betty L. Welsh, "An Interdisciplinary Systems Approach to Accountability," Social Work in Education, 1 (July 1979), pp. 44-54.

11. Elizabeth Timberlake, Chris Anlauf Sabatino, and Sally North Hooper, "Decisions Made in Educational Placement of Handicapped Children," Journal of Social Service Research, 3 (Summer 1979), pp. 187-200.

12. Lewis W. Carr, "NASW Report on Survey of Social Work Services in Schools" (Washington, D.C.: National Association of Social Workers, 1976), (mimeographed); and Paula Allen Meares, "Analysis of Tasks in School Social Work," Social Work, 22 (May 1977), pp. 196-201.

13. The thirteen listed services related to implementing the IEP were: casework counseling to the child; casework counseling to the parent; family group counseling; work with child in group; consultation to the teacher; consultation to the parent; work with parents in group; direct intervention in the classroom; coordination and service integration with community resources; coordination and service integration within the school; liaison role between home and school; action to obtain needed services for the child; mediation between parents and the school system; and other.

14. The definitions of models in statements 1, 2, 3, and 5 were derived from John J. Alderson, "Models of School Social Work Practice," in Rosemary Sarri and Frank Maple, eds., The School in the Community (Washington, D.C.: National Association of Social Workers, 1972), pp. 57-74. Definitions in statements 4 and 6 were derived from Lela B. Costin, "School

Social Work Practice: A New Model," Social Work, 20 (March 1975), pp. 135-139. Acknowledgment and appreciation are extended to Paula Mintzies, who used a similar set of definitions to derive data on models in her unpublished study concerning functions school social workers performed in selected ESAA-funded school districts during school year 1978-79.

15. The seventeen listed functions were: participation in the process of locating children who may be handicapped; psychosocial study and assessment of children who may be handicapped; participation in planning for the IEP; implementation of the IEP; due process mediation, liaison between home and school; coordination and service integration within the school district; promoting the coordination and integration of school services with community based services; implementation of due process provision of P.L. 94-142; evaluation of achievement of objectives; writing reports; consultation with parents; consultation with parents and other school personnel; periodic reviews; preschool screening; leadership role inservice education and training; and leadership and policymaking activities.

16. The fourteen listed concerns were: increased labeling of students; draining of school social work resources away from children needing help through regular education; too much time spent in team meetings; excessive pressure to mainstream; too much time spent related to due process provisions; too much time spent on psychosocial assessments; too much time spent on completion of forms, reports, various paperwork ("red tape"); inadequate funding; social assessments are not prepared for each child considered for or enrolled in special education; social assessments are performed by personnel other than school social workers; needed medical, mental health, and social services are often unavailable "at no cost to the parent"; inappropriate placement of economically poor and/or minority students; not enough student services personnel; and not enough school social workers.

17. "Bureau's Draft Policy on IEPs Leaves Service Provision Gaps," NASW School Social Work Bulletin, March 1980, p. 1.

18. Alderson, op. cit., pp. 62-64.

19. Ibid., pp. 70-73.

20. Elizabeth Timberlake, Chris Anlauf Sabatino, and Sally North Hooper, "School Social Work Practice and P.L. 94-142." Unpublished paper, 1981, p. 31. (Mimeographed.)

21. Paula Meares, "Integrating Systems Intervention and Treatment Approaches in Work with Handicapped Children and Their Families," in Anderson, Freeman, and Edwards, op. cit., pp. 85-86.

SCHOOL SOCIAL WORK PRACTICE:
WHICH WAY THE FUTURE?

Elizabeth M. Timberlake, Chris Anlauf Sabatino,
and Sally North Hooper

Two federal laws, the 1975 Education for All Handicapped Children Act (P.L. 94-142) and the 1980 Community Mental Health Systems Act, hold promise of great impact on children and on the professionals who serve them. The older law mandates educational support services for children with handicapping conditions in order that they may be educated in the least restrictive educational environment possible. Thus, this law suggests expanded professional services for children under the auspices of the public school system. By contrast, the more recently enacted law provides for fewer direct community mental health services for children and no longer mandates children's services as part of community mental health centers. Although the centers are mandated to provide coordinated systems of care for the mentally ill, service energy is directed toward only medical-psychiatric problems and away from children and families under stress or in distress. Thus, the mental health law suggests contraction of community-based children's programs which may have been providing behind-the-scene services and enabling the public schools to educate many children within least restrictive educational environments. By inference, it seems possible that the mental health law will encourage expansion of school social work services as it defaults in meeting community needs. This confusion about whether social-emotional services for school-age children are expanding or contracting is even further complicated by "Reaganomics" or the Reagan administration's emphasis on cutting human service programs in order to balance the nation's budget.

In view of these external federal pressures on future professional services for children, school social workers are reevaluating their own roles in providing services to children within the educational system and in collaborating with the mental health system. To that end, this paper seeks to bring together existing empirical data about: (1) how school social workers view their own professional practice within the schools and (2) how community-based mental health professionals view the mental health services provided within the schools.

VIEW FROM WITHIN

A survey of one-third of the nine hundred registrants at the 1978 National Conference of School Social Workers sponsored by the National Association of

Social Workers (NASW) yielded data about current social work practice in the public school systems of thirty-five states. 1/ The eleven practice tasks frequently performed by 60 percent to 79 percent of the respondents formed three distinct dimensions of practice. The first dimension consisted of consultation, short-term counseling, and diagnostic assessment. These tasks, frequently engaged in by three out of four of the respondents, highlight the multidisciplinary team aspects of direct and indirect social service delivery in the schools. The second dimension consisted of individual counseling of children, concrete services, crisis intervention, individual counseling of parents, home visits, and referral. These six tasks, frequently engaged in by two out of three of the respondents, emphasize direct service provision by school social workers. The third dimension consisted of multiple agency collaboration and social case histories. These two tasks, frequently engaged in by three out of five of the respondents, highlighted the date collection and information sharing aspects of social work practice in a school setting.

In addition to these frequently performed practice tasks, one out of three of the school social work respondents sometimes performed five other tasks: policy and program development, education of school system personnel, family counseling, community organization, and long-term counseling. These tasks supplement and broaden the practice dimension of direct service provision and add an administrative or developmental dimension.

Factor analysis of the twenty-one practice activities under consideration revealed that the respondents varied as to the frequency with which they performed four dimensions of school social work practice. Accounting for 80.4 percent of the variance, this divergence suggested that the practice models of the respondents differentially emphasized treatment activity, resource development activity, family system treatment activity, and multidisciplinary activity. But, did the respondents perceive stability or change in their practice models in relation to the implementation of P.L. 94-142? Half or more noted continued and stable use of the twenty-one practice tasks under consideration. A small percentage perceived a decrease in five long-term treatment tasks. At least one out of three of the respondents identified an increase in seven other tasks: usage of diagnostic assessment, social case history, consultation, multiple agency collaboration, education of personnel, and policy-program development.

VIEW FROM WITHOUT

A survey of one-fourth of the eight hundred child mental health professionals attending the 1978 annual program meeting of the American Association of Psychiatric Services for Children (AAPSC) provided data about mental health services in the public schools as perceived by professionals outside of the school system. 2/ This conference was chosen as it represented the only national multidisciplinary organization of child mental health services and professionals in the United States. Ninety-five percent of the respondents had earned advanced academic degrees. Representing ten mental health disciplines, they practiced in thirty-five states.

Four out of five of the AAPSC respondents thought that mental health services should be universally provided for all children if mental health services for children were to be provided by the public schools. One out of three thought that mental health services should be provided directly by the public schools when therapy was indicated to aid a child's educational adjustment. Half thought that the public schools should finance mental health services provided by mental health clinics when therapy for a child was recommended by the schools.

Three out of four of the respondents perceived the quality of the mental health services offered by the public schools to be inadequate. Over half thought that professionals outside of the school system did not recognize the mental health services currently provided by school as mental health services. Despite the perceived inadequacies, three out of four of the AAPSC respondents thought there should be an increase in the provision of mental health services by the public schools. Over half thought that P.L. 94-142 would result in the public school assuming a larger and more direct role in the mental health of children.

Although respondents agreed that there should be an increase in the provision of mental health services by the public schools, the respondents differed about the appropriateness of specific mental health practice tasks. Four out of five thought it appropriate for school personnel to perform three tasks: problem assessment and referral, group counseling to children related to school adjustment, and individual counseling to children related to school adjustment. Two out of three deemed diagnostic evaluations and outreach services as appropriate. By contrast, only one out of three respondents thought that school personnel should provide individual, family, and group therapy.

IMPLICATIONS OF THE DATA

Since the passage of P.L. 94-142, mental health professionals in the public schools and in community settings have become increasingly aware of the law's provision for counseling services to facilitate the educational progress of school-age children. Both groups hotly debate whether or not the school system should employ community-based mental health professionals to provide counseling services if the school system is unable to budget for such services within its own staff composition. Some school systems have hired their own social workers and other mental health professionals to fulfill the counseling requirements of the law. Yet when these employees seek to meet the mental health needs of targeted groups of children, the school system does not always support such a practice activity as part of their work assignment. That is, counseling tasks are sanctioned by the school system as long as these tasks are performed in addition to their other assignments which are perceived as more educationally oriented.

This double message about task and role presents problems for both school-employed and community-based mental health professionals alike and may explain why the AAPSC respondents viewed school-based mental health

18

services as inadequate and why NASW respondents perceived a decrease in long-term treatment tasks. In other words, the school system's own conflict about the use and role of its mental health employees appears to be reflected in the larger mental health community whose professionals do not know either what school social workers do or what their own supplemental role should be.

The factor analysis of the items about school provision of mental health services further supports the idea of confusion among school-employed and community-based mental health professionals in that 84.3 percent of the variance among AAPSC respondents was accounted for by questions pertaining to provision of mental health services and tasks by the public schools.

Historically, school systems have always assessed the problems encountered by their pupils and responded with a variety of support services clearly related to the school performance problems. Yet school systems traditionally have not viewed mental health services as fitting with their primary goal of educating children. In keeping with the school system's traditional approach, community-based mental health practitioners appear to favor provision of mental health services by school employees only as long as such services remain within the accustomed domain of the educational institution. Community-based mental health professionals tend to view child problems which require therapy as their own particular turf. In part, this split between what are perceived as appropriate and nonappropriate support services within the educational system appears related to the fact that community-based mental health professionals tend not to have a practice model which incorporates knowledge and techniques of intervention in relation to those institutional impingements which can produce developmental or chronic mental health problems among school children.

Historically, there has been little alignment of the school social worker, or other school-employed mental health professionals, with the functioning of an individual school and its own staff in relation to educating children. The data from the NASW study, however, suggest that the increased offering of consultation services by school social workers is pulling the school social worker toward other school employees as a fellow team member also concerned with a pupil's educational dysfunction.

Given the data that indicate both movement toward a view of school social workers as team staff members and away from long-term intensive treatment, the finding that school policy-program development and education of personnel are the two tasks sometimes performed by the highest percentage of school social workers takes on added significance. This finding suggests a movement toward disseminating school social workers' expertise into all areas of the school system, staff, and programs as well as into school system decision-making about pupil dysfunction. It seems possible that these tasks of policy-program development and education of personnel may begin to serve as a bridge between an inaccurate image of the school social worker as a misplaced mental health clinician and a more accurate image of the school social worker as a team expert on the interface between persons and environments. It is also possible that these tasks may help to bridge the gap between school-employed and community-based mental health professionals.

In view of social work's problems of self-definition, it is a distinct accomplishment for the school system to view social work as a profession which has information valuable to every level of the school's organizational structure. In addition, the perceived increase since the passage of P.L. 94-142 in the twenty-one practice tasks under consideration suggests a substantial expansion in the repertoire of generic social work tasks which school social workers include in their daily practice. The tasks most often perceived as increasing are those which involve diagnosing handicapping conditions, giving the system feedback about the data collected during the diagnostic process, and collaboration with community agencies to provide needed services. These findings clearly point to the growing interprofessional team role which school social workers associate with P.L. 94-142. The small increase and the corresponding decrease in long-term treatment tasks which the NASW respondents associated with P.L. 94-142 suggested that the early phase of the implementation of the law has continued the historical trend in school social work practice away from long-term treatment tasks. Since the law mandates the availability of counseling services to handicapped children, this finding was surprising

CONCLUSION

The combined data about how school social workers view their own practice within the schools and how community-based mental health professionals view the mental health services provided within the schools suggest that both groups perceive a core dimension of school social work practice consisting of tasks which support the educational functioning of the school child.

The data presented here also seem to indicate that the core of school social work services has been stable despite external pressures (such as P.L. 94-142) and indicate the integrity of school social work practice and the ability of school social workers to evolve and develop their professional identity in the face of change.

Although the two groups share similar views on school-based mental health activities, this perception is likely to change given the passage of the 1980 Community Mental Health Systems Act and the Reagan block grant proposals for education. No one is able to predict the outcome of these policy decisions. However, it is clear that new pressures will be placed on the school and the community mental health center. These pressures will alter service delivery patterns and availability of services to targeted populations. One of the pressures is likely to be an intense competition among service providers for the limited federal funds.

Professionals who provide services to children and their families will need to move beyond the competition inherent in professional practice and develop a collaborative approach to equitable securement of funding for service delivery. In the face of reduced federal funds, collaboration is no longer a luxury. It is critical to the survival of all public services to children and their families. Without coalitions of community-based and school-based mental health practitioners, mental health clinics will limp along with greatly constricted services, school will eliminate social work positions, and children will suffer the consequences.

NOTES AND REFERENCES

1. Elizabeth M. Timberlake, Chris Anlauf Sabatino, and Sally North Hooper, "School Social Work Practice and P.L. 94-142." Publication in process.

2. Chris Anlauf Sabatino, Elizabeth M. Timberlake, and Sally North Hooper, "Issues Related to the Interface Between Mental Health Services and Public Schools." Publication in process.

COMPREHENSIVE SCHOOL SOCIAL WORK
ASSESSMENT OF CHILDREN

Robert J. Gallagher

The comprehensive school social work assessment of children is one of the most crucial issues facing school social work today. The mandates of P.L. 94-142 combined with the current political climate require school social workers to review their service delivery with an eye toward the refinement of standards and guidelines. 1/ The providing of social assessment is certainly one of those areas of service delivery which has a significant impact on the type of education children receive. It is the intent of this article to address the following elements of the comprehensive school social work assessment of children:

1. A discussion of some of the more complex issues surrounding the assessment of children.

2. Laying down some basic "givens" to be used in defining the parameters of child assessment.

3. Looking at some of the elements which need to be included in the assessment of children.

4. Thoughts on the outcome of child assessment.

The author is very aware that any small portion of this paper could contain enough useful and fertile ground for volumes of books. It is not my intention to present exhaustive discussion of the topic but rather to lay some common groundwork.

What is to be shared in this paper is neither new nor revolutionary. Indeed, the philosophy of this article is easily recognizable as coming from the common base of social work knowledge. 2/ What then is the purpose of filling the following pages with information which is embedded in the literature of our profession? Primarily, because the profession has not done an adequate job of pulling the various elements together and applying them to social work in the schools; and most important: letting others know what school social workers are doing.

A major issue confronting the school social worker in the assessment of children, is deciding how much is enough or where to stop. While P.L. 94-142 appears to be rather specific about what are considered to be the essential elements involved in such an assessment, in reality, the interpretation of what meets the needs of a child varies widely from one state to another and from one school district to another. Some few places do require a complete, comprehensive school social work assessment on every child referred for any service. In those areas, the decision of the school social worker is simplified. Every child receives the same type of evaluation and the school social worker is there almost exclusively for evaluations. While this may provide good job security for school social work and chisel out any easily definable territory, there are some who question the wisdom of allocating limited staff time in this manner.

In other areas, the limitations on staff and resources combined with the mandate for additional services to be provided by school social workers have left the school social workers with a great deal of discretionary power for determining the extent of school social work assessment each child receives. The depth of assessment in these areas is appropriately based on the degree and intensity of the presenting problem. This criterion relies chiefly upon the results of consultation with the referring party (usually a parent or teacher); a review of the cumulative folder for information on past difficulties or social and emotional problems; and the observation of the child. Based upon the results of these investigations, the school social worker then determines whether or not a more comprehensive evaluation is appropriate. The main criterion utilized in this determination in most cases is the child's ability to relate effectively with the systems to feel good about himself or herself. Should problems be identified in any of these areas, a more detailed assessment is usually indicated. While this appears to be more or less the process that most school social workers go through in determining the depth of assessment, there remains a need for this process to be standardized and guidelines developed for decision making.

GENERAL PARAMETERS

The following are some assumptions which should be regarded as general parameters in the comprehensive assessment of children. All the elements presented here need to be considered within the context of comprehensive team evaluation. School social workers must realize the strength of the team concept in providing comprehensive services. The interplay among team members and the cooperative spirit developed on the team, especially with regard to issues of territoriality, can put services to children eons ahead of areas in which there is either no team or a dysfunctioning team. 3/

A significant portion of school social workers' responsibility to the diagnostic team and to the child lies in their ability to specify and fulfill their role. Writing about the relationship of social work to other professions, Boehm states the following:

> A domain of the specialized knowledge must develop which will furnish the theoretical underpinnings for the practice skills by which the profession expresses its function. Each profession has a specific or core function and in a sense, holds a monopoly on this function, however, each profession shares with all other professions in society a type of village green, a common area that is peripheral to each profession. 4/

Indeed, school social workers do have much common ground with other professionals in pupil personnel work. This makes it even more essential that social workers become articulate in describing what they do and how they do it. It is in this context that an understanding needs to be developed among team members with regard to specific role functions. For example, the information presented in this article is information which all school social workers can consider in making a determination upon the relative social functioning of a child. However, the actual gathering of this information can, and indeed in most cases is, the responsibility of more than just the school social worker. Much of this information is appropriately gathered by the school nurse, or the psychologist, or through the classroom teacher. Information gathered by a competent, well-functioning assessment team, is gathered in such a way that its usefulness is relevant to all members of the team. It is certainly the function of the school social worker to provide the team with an assessment of the social impact of all relevant information. Another general parameter is that the real cornerstone of all assessments is professional judgment. Used properly, this judgment has the power to convert an assortment of graphs, numbers, and scores into descriptors of vibrant relationships with all their interplay and energy. But for professional judgment to be used properly, it must be used with a sound comprehension of its limitations.

In and of itself, professional judgment is not a substitute for any aspect of the comprehensive assessment. Professional judgment is vital in determining the limitations of an assessment; how much is enough, what is relevant, and what is not. However, to make a decision for placement or nonplacement or to provide or deny services on the basis of professional judgment alone without substantiating data is the worst kind of misuse of power and responsibility. School social workers on an assessment team have a responsibility to be able to substantiate their judgment with objective data. This is the role of professional judgment; to be used as a valuable guide in the determination of what information needs to be gathered, how to gather it, and what it means.

SYSTEMS APPROACH

The basic frame of reference for the assessment is the systems approach. 5/ This approach is being utilized for a number of reasons. First, it is all encompassing and not only allows for the application of any theoretical framework but enhances it. Secondly, the systems approach helps the school social worker to keep a perspective and avoids the assumption that the "child is the problem," while still making it possible to keep the child as the focus of assessment. But it does allow for approaches which can target other elements in the child's life as sharing in responsibility for change. The systems approach disseminates problem ownership and allows for a more creative and more powerful solution to difficulties. Third, the systems approach is humbling in its scope; it keeps social workers from becoming too caught up in their power to bring about change by themselves by its own immense power.

One of the possible difficulties in utilizing the systems approach lies in its vastness. It is easy to become so immersed in a system that you lose sight of your purpose for being there. However, the systems approach offers a solution to this problem. That solution is boundaries. Even a comprehensive school social work evaluation has real and appropriate boundaries. These boundaries lie in a clear understanding of the focus, context, and guiding principles of the evaluation. (See Figure 1.) The focus is "the child," the context is "in education," and the guiding principle is "educational relevancy." It is by keeping a clear eye on these boundaries that school social workers can avoid the pitfall of assessment gobbledygook wherein they stray into areas which are neither educationally relevant nor a legitimate concern of the school system.

The following is a discussion of the specific elements of the assessment itself. It should be remembered that while specifics will be mentioned in various aspects of this article, they are mentioned only as examples. They should not be considered the end all and the be all, indeed there is much more which could be considered.

The Child

While an assessment may begin appropriately in a number of different systems, this article will begin with the child as the focus. While the initial referral in a vast majority of cases is initiated either through the school or the family, the child's view of the difficulty is essential to a comprehensive evaluation. This view can be evolved in a number of ways; the most comfortable for the child is frequently a structured interview in which a child is given a basic understanding of the assessment process and in which his or her questions and concerns are elicited. The child's view of himself or herself, while coming through in all aspects of a comprehensive assessment, is not something that should be left solely to inferences from other elements of the assessment. The child's direct view of the situation frequently contains more than a small amount of insight into possible solutions. There are also many instruments available which allow children to present their concerns about themselves and their world.

The Primary Self-Concept Inventory, Piers-Harris, and the Coopersmith can all give reliable pictures of the child's self-view. The California Test of Personality is a powerful instrument to gather a child's view of the many aspects of his or her relationships with family, school, and peers. Sentence completion allows an opportunity for a more introspective look at the many emotions and realities with which the child copes. All of these can assist the school social worker in utilizing professional judgment in such a way so as to objectify and measure some very important aspects of the child being assessed.

The Family

A natural progression following or in connection with elicitation of the child's view next involves the family system. Bearing in mind the system's natural anxiety over identifying one of its own members as having a difficulty, it is frequently advantageous to start with relatively neutral ground. A social history has traditionally provided the profession of

Fig. 1. Components and Relationships in the Systems Approach.

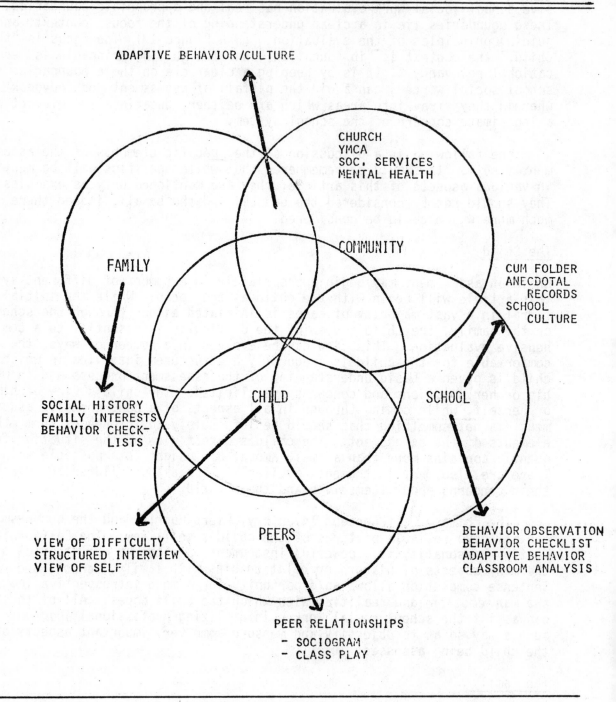

ADAPTIVE BEHAVIOR/CULTURE

CHURCH
YMCA
SOC. SERVICES
MENTAL HEALTH

COMMUNITY

FAMILY

CUM FOLDER
ANECDOTAL
RECORDS
SCHOOL
CULTURE

SOCIAL HISTORY
FAMILY INTERESTS
BEHAVIOR CHECK-
LISTS

CHILD

SCHOOL

VIEW OF DIFFICULTY
STRUCTURED INTERVIEW
VIEW OF SELF

PEERS

BEHAVIOR OBSERVATION
BEHAVIOR CHECKLIST
ADAPTIVE BEHAVIOR
CLASSROOM ANALYSIS

PEER RELATIONSHIPS
- SOCIOGRAM
- CLASS PLAY

social work with a vital tool for assisting in the formation of a comprehensive picture of an individual. A good developmental social history encompasses the following: significant parental information such as age, health, and pertinent background; a child's prenatal history; birth history; early developmental milestones; preschool health; relationship patterns with parents, siblings, and peers; educational history; perceived strengths and needs; relative interests, hobbies, or sports; response to correction; involvement with community agencies; major illness or trauma; and current health status. 6/

All of these data can be powerful aids for determining whether a specific learning problem is developmental, educational, or behavioral-emotional in nature. Such information is vital, as the appropriate remediation for each may vary significantly. An additional variable that a comprehensive developmental social history can provide is documentation about the presence or absence of the duration of a problem which again provides the educator with useful programming information. In many instances, a developmental social history is supplemented by a diagnostic family interview for the purpose of assessing current family relationships. A frequently used structure for this interview is the "typical day" format in which the family guides the interviewer through their typical day as they see it. 7/ The interplay of the relationships quickly becomes apparent in this format and it allows for a sound understanding of the family dynamics to develop. Not only does the family participate in the formulation of the diagnosis in this way, but also the potential is present for utilizing the typical-day interview as a basis for later intervention if appropriate. It should be emphasized here that child assessment can and should be to some extent a therapeutic process that can allow for a smooth transitional flow from assessment to intervention or perhaps be sufficiently therapeutic in and of itself so as to eliminate the need for further intervention.

Nonbiased Data

One of the greatest values of P.L. 94-142 lies in its mandating of nonbiased objective data to be utilized in the assessment of children. The gathering of these data can go a long way toward assisting a reluctant family or school to the appropriate identification of a difficulty. Behavioral checklists have been found to be an invaluable tool not only in the identification of, but in the acceptance of, the existing difficulties. There are many types of behavioral checklist data; some of them, such as the Devereux, the Burks, or the Quail, are commercially available; others are developed locally to identify specific local needs. Though the formats differ somewhat, they generally have a "significant other" such as a parent or teacher respond to various behavioral descriptors and note whether such behaviors are a problem, and if so, to what degree. While some such as Burks rely on face validity (a rating of 5 on a scale of 1 to 5 indicates a very significant problem), others such as the Devereux have the added advantage of being normed on residential populations as well as regular school populations.

The advantages to these scales are many, not the least of which is that they can begin the therapeutic process of owning a problem by recognizing its existence. The profiles presented by these ratings are more often than not a reliable image of the relationship patterns between a child and the parents as well as between a child and a group of teachers. The advantage of having both parents and a number of teachers complete the scales becomes readily apparent to the social worker interested in helping all involved understand the similarities and differences of how a child relates to different systems. A further advantage of the behavior scales is their usefulness in identifying the frequency of behavioral difficulties as well as the relative intensity of these difficulties.

The Community

Crossing the boundaries between the child and family system as they interface with the community allows for a look at how a child copes with the roles placed upon him or her by the family and the community as seen through the child's adaptive behavior. The assessment of this adaptive behavior is done through the utilizing of appropriate instruments such as the SOMPA, the AAMD, or the Vineland. These instruments are not designed specifically for problem identification so much as identifying how a child is mastering life functions as compared to other similar children. These scores are normed on appropriate populations; some, such as SOMPA, according to age, sex, and cultural background; others (such as the AAMD) according to age, sex, intelligence, or program placement. These scales are among the most researched and validated rating scales available today, and unlike behavioral problem checklists, adaptive behavior scales are also valuable in the identification of areas of relative strength as well as weaknesses. 8/ This knowledge can be invaluable in the process of developing an IEP for a child.

To further assess the interfacing of the child, family, and community, a determination can be made, with the family, of the family support systems utilized in the community. These may include the church, the YMCA, and social services, mental health, or other community agencies. This information can be valuable when it comes to assessing (1) the family's ability to cope with demands placed upon it, (2) the child and family support systems, and (3) willingness of the family to become involved beyond its specific boundaries. Additionally, a sometimes highly significant factor is a comparison between the family's cultural atmosphere, that of the community, and that of the school. Frequently, when a child's cultural base is significantly different from the predominant culture of the school, adaptations in educational programming become appropriate.

The School

The child should also be viewed within the school as a system. This is an area where frequently the objectivity of the assessor is put to the test. School social workers have a direct professional (as well as sometimes financial) commitment to the school as a system, and they sometimes become so immersed within its workings that they can fail to view it objectively. While it may take a significant amount of courage to consider the politics of the school, the interplay between principal, teacher, and significant others, and the general atmosphere of the school and its direct effect upon any one child within the system, it is on occasion very necessary.

One of the basic elements of an assessment available to the social worker is information documented in the cumulative folder. While this information can frequently provide a good deal of insight--especially into the history and duration of specific difficulties--one must bear in mind that cumulative folders also frequently contain much biased and prejudicial information about a child, and such information should be viewed critically. The same holds true for anecdotal records; while their usefulness should not be underrated (and indeed would not be by anyone utilizing a well-kept anecdotal log), a truly objective, nonprejudicial anecdotal log can be somewhat of a rarity.

An absolutely vital portion of any comprehensive child assessment is direct behavioral observation. To be truly comprehensive, such data should be gathered in structured settings such as reading or math class as well as in unstructured settings such as recess or lunch. With information provided not only on how the child being assessed and other children respond to their environment and the adults but also on how that environment and the adults respond to the child, behavioral observation then becomes a dynamic assessment tool.

Another important element of a truly comprehensive assessment is that of classroom analysis. While being relatively new in terms of assessing its impact on a specific child, classroom analysis can be invaluable in delineating the strengths and weaknesses of the classroom system and in providing a wealth of fertile ground for IEP intervention. 9/ An area that is frequently overlooked in the assessment of children is the gathering of data on peer relationships. It is somewhat ironic that social workers either overlook this area or tend to assess it by inference ("I think Billy is rejected by his peers").

Research tells us that the opinions of peers are more reliable than those of parents, teachers, psychiatrists, or social workers, especially when assessing social functioning. 10/ Undoubtedly, part of the absence of peer data in an assessment is due to the difficulty in measurement that such information presents in light of the needs for confidentiality during such an assessment. However, if social workers would look to their roots they would find the methods by which social scientists have been measuring peer interaction for many decades--the sociogram. The information derived from this instrument can go a long way toward establishing the degree to which an individual is accepted or rejected, as well as providing a wealth of information on how his or her peers function as a system.

Even more valuable information is available from a device entitled "The Class Play," which is a listing of twelve roles (such as the leader, the bully, someone with a good sense of humor, and so forth) for which each child picks the person in the room he or she thinks could best play that role. 11/ The children then pick the roles they would like to play, the roles they think the teacher would like them to play, and the roles they think their peers would pick for them. These roles can then be tabulated to produce such information as (1) how a child's peers perceive his or her strengths and weaknesses, (2) whether the child's perception of how he or she is viewed by peers is accurate, (3) what the child perceives as his or her own strengths and weaknesses, or (4) what positive roles the child would like to play. This can all be valuable information, especially in connection with a child who has an inaccurate picture of himself or herself and wants to change it to a more positive role.

As can be seen, the elements which can be involved in a truly comprehensive assessment of a child by a school social worker can indeed become numerous and voluminous. There are certainly additional elements which in various cases may be very appropriate to educational assessment. However, in the vast majority of cases, the degree of assessment would be significantly less than that which is described here.

EDUCATIONAL RELEVANCE

The assessment itself is not truly complete until it has been put together in an educationally relevant manner. Here again is where one finds the usefulness of appropriate professional judgment. The main criterion to be used for a comprehensive assessment is the guiding principle of "educational relevance." Assessments completed by a school social worker do not yield scores directly related to cognitive functioning such as IQ or achievement scores. The information in a school social worker's assessment relates directly to the affective behavioral domain and the worker's job, therefore, is to give an understanding of the direct relationship between how a child is feeling and what he or she is capable of learning.

It is the school social worker's function after completing an assessment to act as a filter in determining what should go into the final write-up, what is an appropriate diagnosis, what are educationally meaningful IEP goals, and perhaps most vitally, what are some concrete, pragmatic avenues of intervention. The social worker must show, for example, that Jane's fear of failure is a determining factor in her inability to complete tasks; that Mike's desire to maintain his role as a class clown is greater than his desire to read effectively and that until he channels or redefines his role his difficulties will continue. These are real-life, educationally significant results which can be gleaned from a comprehensive school social work assessment.

It is especially vital that written reports be free of bias and prejudicial data. This carries added importance when viewed within the provisions of the Family Right to Privacy Act. If a child's father's history of mental illness has no direct educational relevance to the child's functioning in the classroom, then it has no business being in a report assessing that functioning. It is sometimes helpful to look at the various elements of information gathered in an assessment as if it were on a continuum from educational relevance to educational nonrelevance. The two poles of the continuum which can be thought of graphically as either black or white, allow for an immediate determination of whether something should be included in a report. The difficulty comes in the center of the continuum, where there is a gray area. It is information in this area that sometimes demands every bit of tact and diplomacy that school social workers can muster. Whether it relates to an incestuous relationship within the family or political interplay between the principal and teacher, the decision of whom to share such information with could tax the best professional judgment.

But just as the information itself can be viewed on a continuum, the dissemination of that information can be viewed as being on a continuum, with one end being complete nonreporting and the other end being a complete and thorough written evaluation. The middle ground, therefore, represents different degrees stretching all the way from the school social worker retaining and observing the situation, to sharing it in a confidential manner with the classroom teacher, or taking any other intermediate, appropriate steps.

It is readily apparent that a truly comprehensive assessment can be very time consuming and require a broad cross section of assessment skills. This emphasizes the need to progress quickly toward the development of guidelines to be used in the determination of which children receive what degree of comprehensive assessment. While not all children would be in need of an equally comprehensive assessment, for those children who have social deficits, the social assessment is invaluable in the development of IEP goals and intervention strategies. It is, therefore, encouraging to see the interest being generated on the local and national levels around the issue of assessment and its value in determining services for children.

NOTES AND REFERENCES

1. Lynda Treger, "A Model for Psychosocial Assessment," School Social Work Quarterly, 3 (Fall 1979).

2. Hariett M. Bartlett, Common Base of Social Work Practice (New York: National Association of Social Workers, 1970).

3. Richard J. Anderson, "School Social Work: The Promise of a Team Model," Child Welfare, 54 (October 1974).

4. Werner W. Boehm, "Relationship of Social Work to Other Professions," Encyclopedia of Social Work (15th issue; New York: National Association of Social Workers, 1965), p. 641.

5. Ralph E. Anderson and Irl Carter, A Human Systems Syllabus (Adeline, 1973).

6. Dianne L. Henry, Joyce DeChristopher, Pat Dowling, and E. Virginia Lapham, "Using the Social History to Assess Handicapping Conditions," Social Work in Education, 3 (April 1981), pp. 7-19.

7. Sherry Lynn Fears, "Adlerian Parent Study Groups," The School Counselor (May 1976).

8. Daniel J. Reschly, "Workshop Outline, Special Study Institute on Adaptive Behavior," Iowa Department of Public Instruction, Division of Special Education, Ames, Iowa, 1980; "Adaptive Behavior: Background, Assessment, and Practice," Psychology Department, Iowa State University, Ames, Iowa, mimeographed.

9. Dean H. Nielsen and Diana H. Kirk, "Evaluating Educational Performance," Classroom Climates.

10. N. Phillips Beeman and M. Vere DeVault, "Relation of Positive and Negative Sociometric Valuations to Social and Personal Adjustment of School Children," Journal of Applied Psychology, 39 (1955).

11. Eli M. Bower, Early Identification of Emotionally Handicapped Children In School, (Springfield, Ill.: Charles C Thomas, 1960).

In preparing this article, the author received assistance from members of NASW's Council on Social Work Services in Schools and from Irv Forester, school social worker, and George Harper, school psychologist.

MARKETABLE SOCIAL WORK SKILLS

CLAIRE B. GALLANT

In today's money-crunch approach to society's problems, social workers must be able to present themselves in a positive way that spells economy. Business and other professionals frequently oversell themselves, while social workers undersell themselves. In an economic weary world, social workers must articulate their skills which are marketable.

Coming out of an idealistic, humanistic philosophy, social workers do not vigorously assert their expertise. No one in the profession likes braggarts; however, due to the emphasis our nation places on marketing, advertising, and selling, the profession's image must change. The general public and community decision makers must be made aware of social work's attributes in specific terms--skills which are profitable in money and time, as well as in human endeavors. Social workers are human engineers, family architects, social educators, and social process facilitators. They must claim their unique abilities and sell themselves consciously as human process experts. No other profession puts together human beings and social systems in the way social work is able to do. The school social worker cannot take away the pain of having a handicapped child, but he or she is able to help the parents and school work toward a proper solution for the child. The skills in providing this help need to be articulated. Social workers are drawn to their profession often for humanitarian and idealistic reasons. They are in a service-oriented profession.

In order to explain the profession's processes so decision makers understand why a case went well, the social worker must consciously force explanations. Some procedures that practitioners do automatically, such as introducing people, paying attention to what someone is saying, or looking at them directly, seem like simple suggestions when they are a part of one's procedures. The author's observations of some meetings illustrate this does not always happen. The worker who truly respects human beings will be courteous. The in-service that is now offered to school administrators trains them in some of these procedures.

In a recent special study institute entitled Improving Communication Skills for Chairpersons, the participants were to learn the following skills:

1. Learn to control the flow of discussion, including (a) skills of summary, (b) drawing out quiet members, and (c) curtailing irrelevant comments.

2. Practice various communication skills, including (a) paraphrasing, (b) perception checks, (c) behavior descriptions, and (d) description of feelings.

3. Develop techniques for conflict resolution and fostering consensus decision making.

Now, school social workers in the towns where these school administrators work could easily demonstrate and teach these skills. However, they often do not vigorously assert their knowledge and articulate their skills. School social work department heads and consultants describe their pride to the author when her training is introduced into their respective states. "So often," they say, "it is others lecturing to us."

It is essential that the profession use social work theory to illustrate why it engages in specific processes. It is then important to break down the process to demonstrate correct procedures and accountability. Accountability and outcomes must be tied to an evaluation of the process. Social workers are then able to explain their behavior and tie their various phases of operation together.

The author, in order to teach, train, and explain the concept of mediation to trainees under the federal grant entitled "Using Social Work Skills in Due Process Mediation Procedures under P.L. 94-142," used the following outline:

PHASES IN MEDIATION

I. Introductory Phase.

    A. Introductions.
    B. Rules of order.
    C. Due process procedures.

II. Assessment Phase.

    A. Parents' presentation of their views.
    B. School's presentation of its views.

III. Trust Building and Clarifying Phase.

    A. Questions and clarifications of issues by mediator.
    B. Allowing both sides to present views.
    C. Go over IEPs and minutes of official school and parents' meeting.

IV. Problem Solving and Negotiation Phase.

    A. Separate sessions or caucus to gauge where both sides are or to clarify ideas.
    B. State or write and read consensus ideas both in caucus or in total group.

C. Point out movement or lack of movement.
D. Keep focus on student's needs.

V. Contract Phase.

A. After consensus is agreed to, write in specific terms.
B. Read out loud as well as letting both sides read statements.
C. Carefully include timelines, monitoring, and facilitator in order to enhance contract's workability.

These phases in procedures are coordinated with a videotape presentation, as well as to the detailed observer's assessment sheet. Now, no one would have to instruct an experienced school social worker to "sit between the parent and school personnel or across from both, and never to be blocked off from anyone's view." However, if you have only sat behind a desk or taught a class, these simple techniques may not be known to you. This is particularly true during the time of tension or hostility. In the trust-building phase, for example, the question is asked, "Is all the written material displayed openly?" Anyone who has worked in a school knows how jealously some professionals guard their materials. Parents constantly feel intimidated by reports filled with jargon and ominous-sounding phrases. (The author's use of IEP is a good case in point, but parents have learned these initials.)

Where but from social work philosophy would the following observation be important--"If in a successful mediation everyone wins, in an education mediation, the child should gain the most. Give examples in the written contract of that happening."

The next training procedure the author developed is entitled "Process Points for Mediators." They are broken down into an external and internal format with an evaluation or outcome section which is the written contract. Many of the points are social work skills that are incorporated into mediation.

PROCESS POINTS FOR MEDIATORS

External:

1. Greet both sides as quickly as possible. Be warm and polite but conscious that your every movement, word and look is observed by both sides.

2. Put both sides at ease as quickly as possibly by being on time, stating ground rules in a direct, specific, informal approach.

3. State due process or appeal procedures clearly and seriously.

4. By mediator's posture, position at table, speech and confidence, it is made clear that mediator is in charge of session.

Internal:

5. Assess situation by requesting parents to tell the problem from their perspective.

6. Further assess situation by school personnel's presentation of problem and reasons for judgments. Ask clarifying questions. Cut through long discourses. Read IEP or planning minutes for yourself. Be sure parents have seen everything. Make this very visible.

7. Gauge how far apart the sides are by statements and attitudes (body language, facial grimaces, what is not said, tone, and so forth).

8. Caucus or see each group separately if you feel you are not getting the whole picture, or for a cooling-off period if tension is high.

9. Keep process focused on present and future by your questions or statements if necessary. Keep returning to child's program needs.

10. Test out by tentative summing up or clarifying statements when material is repetitious or there is no movement.

11. Write nonjargon, explicit sentences of agreement as negotiation takes place and read to both sides for clarification. Read separately if there is wide disagreement.

Contract Writing: (Outcomes)

12. Simple, clear statements.

13. Specify dates of meetings between parents and school personnel at regular intervals.

14. Name a contract person or coordinator whom both sides trust, or at the very least, a neutral person.

15. Allow for flexibility of planning by stating alternatives.

In order to meet the challenge that mediation was not a gift or hidden quality, the author spelled out the skills and knowledge required for mediation competency.

SKILLS AND KNOWLEDGE REQUIRED FOR MEDIATION COMPETENCY

A. Detailed Knowledge of Due Process Procedures of P.L. 94-142 and Relevant State Legislation and Regulations.

Specific knowledge of laws, rules, and regulations regarding federal and state special education legislation is a necessary prerequisite in order to guide the mediation process effectively.

B. Knowledge of Special Education Programs and Related Services.

In order to arrive at a correct solution for the child, the mediator must be knowledgeable regarding the range of special education programs and related services. Local school personnel and parents usually have current information available, but it may be interpreted differently. The mediator must be able to question and obtain this information in a systematic way.

C. Skill in Interpersonal Relations and Group Process Management.

As the mediator comes from a power position in the eyes of the parents and school personnel, it is very important not to present an "I know best" attitude. An open, flexible, warm but "in control" approach is usually the preferred one. However, as a group always takes on its own life, the mediator's goal is to manage the group in the best interest of the child. The skill in accomplishing these tasks takes considerable experience and shifting of emphasis, as this is not a therapy group.

Alternatively, mediation can be a catalyst to parents' and school personnel's strengths to overcome their hostilities and work together to help the child.

D. Ability to Understand and Communicate Case Material.

In this mediation model, the mediator does not receive any case material prior to the session. This is done in order to present as unbiased a position as possible. Consequently, the mediator must elicit pertinent data from the parents and school personnel. Essential to a successful mediation is the mediator's skill in perceiving the child's situation. The skill is to communicate the facts so that a proper solution is formulated jointly. There must be a correct assessment of the issues. This is often done in a highly charged atmosphere, which the mediator needs to alleviate, while at the same time not questioning in such a way that defensive participants feel belittled or overlooked.

E. Skill in Clinical Assessment.

Clinical knowledge is a necessary prerequisite for mediation training. As most mediation sessions are conducted in an emotionally charged atmosphere, it is imperative that diagnostic assessments be quickly and accurately arrived at in order to set a tone and direction to the mediation. The traditional approaches must be short-circuited as the time frame does not allow for lengthy formulations.

F. Problem Solving and Ability to Negotiate

The legal system's traditional method of problem solving demands that the parties assume adversarial positions on the premise that out of differences and conflict a just solution will emerge. In contrast, mediation builds from what the parties have in common. Negotiation is a skill that can reinforce a positive, less adversarial, atmosphere.

Negotiation may be characterized as the process by which both sides, guided by the mediator, reach a solution truly satisfactory to all concerned. Negotiation is not "giving in"; its goal is a positive and constructive solution. The mediator must guide the parties to an agreement which utilizes the parties' beliefs and attitudes which are mutually acceptable.

The child's interests must be paramount. Adult hostilities, recounting of past grievances, turf struggles, must all be dealt with, but the goal is to arrive at a suitable program for the child.

G. Contract Writing.

As the contract is the written proof of the mediation's success, it is essential that the contract be a document that can be implemented. The wording should be concise and clear. Several ingredients ought to be present to ensure that the mediation agreement is carried out. Time frames, monitoring devices, and specific personnel are only some of the aspects that need to be examined by the mediator. The therapeutic aspects of contract writing will be discussed and illustrated.

The mediation training under the grant "Using Social Work Skills in Due Process Mediation Procedures under P.L. 94-142" has been received positively by the organizers in the several states that have agreed to the training. However, the participants' enthusiastic response has been documented throughout the country. School social workers must work very hard to maintain themselves as the chief participants. Now, some people may argue with that approach, as everyone wants schools to be more responsive to parents' needs. However, the power position envisioned in any due process procedure by school administrators is very real. Social work is not accustomed to an assignment of a power position in schools. Monmouth County, New Jersey, is piloting a project under the mediation grant to assign school social workers mediation responsibilities throughout the county. (The circumstances around that fact are the basis for another article. However, it is basically strong school social work leadership at all levels, excellently trained and responsive school social work practitioners, and a responsive administration.)

These ingredients of leadership, excellence, and responsiveness need to be present to make any institutional change. Social workers are certainly writing and demonstrating their expertise. 1/ Campbell has drawn attention to using educational tools such as the IEP as a viable method of evaluation. 2/

As a state consultant, the author could speak with authority regarding such school social work competence. However, as a hearing officer and mediator for five years under due process regulations, she was able to observe firsthand the impact of school social work services and the difference they could make, as being intimately involved at a crisis point many guesses become clear.

A breakdown in costs in cases that go on to hearings is estimated at about $1,000 to $1,500 per case in some school districts. Schools estimate sixty to eighty hours of staff time in preparation for a hearing. It is cost-effective to work out alternatives. One workable solution is to utilize school social work services in a preventive approach. There are specific activities and behaviors necessary to lessen the need for expensive unnecessary due process procedures. Some that will be enlarged upon are:

I. Family Involvement.

   A. Nonblaming of parents by school personnel.
   B. Principals and school staff sensitized to parents' grief over a handicapped child.
   C. Positive attention to differences in families.
   D. Parents more aware of difficulties in running a good school.

II. School Atmosphere.

   A. Teachers feeling genuinely worthwhile.
   B. Lessening need to protect turf on school personnel's part.

III. School Procedures.

   A. Early social work involvement with vulnerable, as well as "legally prone" families.
   B. Verbal and written interpretations presented in nonblaming, nonjudgmental style.
   C. Staff development.
   D. Conciliation and mediation responsibilities assigned to school social workers.
   E. Smooth-working liaisons with community agencies.

Although parental involvement is mandated under P.L. 94-142 and many state regulations, it can be stated rather bluntly that there is not a real commitment across the board to what social workers would agree is real parent involvement necessary to achieve this regulation. However, the author's direct observations as a hearing officer and state-appointed mediator only too clearly indicate that parents are often passed over, ignored, and brushed aside. Various patterns in school organization have to change before parents are positively involved. Previously, as a state consultant for school social services in Connecticut, the author worked with Wendy Glasgow Winters at the Martin Luther King School in New Haven, Connecticut. The test for the author came when she observed the comfortable give-and-take behavior between parents and staff--in the teacher's room! All the words became real when this observation repeated itself regularly.

Social workers have the skill to facilitate this positive alliance and trust. When professional school social workers take part in team meetings where parents are blamed or manipulated, it is easy to understand anger on all sides. In cases that go to due process, very frequently it is the lack of attention to what some school personnel would consider "demandingness" on the part of parents--for example, truly being given enough notice in preparation for a meeting. Parents of handicapped children constantly carry internally a tremendous amount of emotion that most of us only touch periodically. If we are feeling fine, a brusque clerk only slightly irritates us, but if we feel resented and unhappy, the occurrence becomes magnified. However, secretaries are assigned various roles in schools and usually reflect administration's attitudes. In a small, affluent town where the author was assigned to do a mediation, in asking for the principal or chief administrator, the receptionist irritably shouted over the loudspeaker, "A parent to see you, Mr. Jones." When she was informed of the correct reason why the principal was needed, her whole attitude changed. Needless to say, when the parents stated their anger at the negative treatment they had received and that that was why they were going to "due process," the author's internal checklist verified the negative responsiveness.

Much of the literature and studies in special education and the field of the handicapped verifies the tremendous grief parents experience. Solnit and Stark pointed out in 1961 how necessary it was to mourn the birth of a defective child. 3/ Patterson writes about a grief model for application within the school. 4/ The tremendous work that is now being done by school social workers in this area in preschool programs around the country is exciting and encouraging. However, the author's own observations continue to illustrate how angry and unsympathetic many school and other professionals are to parents of handicapped children prior to and during litigation. In one community, a school board attorney, in front of the father, blamed the parent for his child's autism, claiming the parents' divorce was responsible. Many equally cruel examples could be cited.

Perhaps when cases go into litigation, people become threatened, but the feelings must be there or they would not be expressed so brutally. How school personnel really feel about handicapped children and their parents needs to be analyzed and explored. School social workers can perform this task better than any other professional without making everybody defensive. Social workers have the theoretical understanding that enables the trust to be established that can lead to a solution. There are parental developmental milestones that can be predicted. No one can or should alleviate grief, but to exacerbate the guilt or angry feelings only leads to more due process procedures.

It must be added here rather emphatically that the author is in no way opposed to mediations or hearings in special education situations. School social workers are all aware that many of their procedures and gains would not be in place if cases were not legally pursued. The problem comes in the situations that are not appropriate. In addition, once a case goes to litigation, feelings and energies are often consumed with the "win or lose" syndrome. School personnel have confessed their discomfort and conflict once a situation becomes a legal case. How an individual protects herself or himself is often very unconscious. One cannot deny the fears on both sides.

STRENGTH OF THE FAMILY

As a delegate to the White House Conference on Families, the author is impressed with the diversities in the American family. Social workers are in a position to assist all school staff in understanding the strengths in families. If single-parent families are judged critically, there will be repercussions. School administrators must be helped to understand not everyone is upwardly mobile. When parents feel judged, they retaliate. A sensitive school administrator told the author his memories of being discriminated against because his lunch bag contained garlic and salami sandwiches. His sensitivity was always present even when some parents were excessively demanding.

In a small school in a rural area of Connecticut, the school personnel pronounced their rejection of "Navy families." At the White House Conference in Baltimore, Maryland, the military families made a special plea for understanding which was very real. The mediator in the case mentioned felt the discrimination against this family. It is often the little side remarks or quiet statements that reveal the true prejudices. School social workers should interpret the strengths of the family. Their anecdotes can be purposely recited.

Another area that needs attention is parents' understanding of what it takes to run a good school. In Greenwich, Connecticut, a system of "parent assisters" has been established. The training was conducted by the author and planned by a parents group and school personnel. These parents, because of this intimacy with school workings, are now more sympathetic to real school problems but astutely aware when they are getting the "runaround" or being ignored. Some of the resistances to this program of parent assisters were internal, particularly some pupil personnel staff as well as some administrators. However, with the superintendent of schools' sanction, the project has been growing. School social workers and principals decide if parents should be referred for the assistance, or parents can refer themselves. A helping natural network is important to stimulate; however, one does have to be a secure professional. Parents are often unaware of the trials and tribulations involved in running a good school. They can help each other objectify the situation which has a direct payoff in decreasing anger and impulsive due process proceedings when they have this understanding.

Another important area to develop is a feeling of being worthwhile as a member of our society and making a contribution. Although the teacher is mandated to be on some teams because of school hierarchy and administrative procedures, he or she is often intimidated by the procedures. Every effort should be made to dissuade this practice. If teachers are truly involved, they can make the most significant link to understanding the child's problem, as well as positively wanting to help the child. The parents are often more involved with the teacher than any other member of the team. If the teacher has no sense of power, this is transmitted to the parent. Often the teacher identifies with the parent, especially if he or she is ignored by school administrators or pupil personnel.

The author's observations frequently illustrate the problem school administrators make for themselves when they ignore making teachers feel genuinely worthwhile. Social work has people like Maple writing about and demonstrating the process of shared decision making. 5/ The author, as school

social work consultant, had training workshops in this process that social
workers, principals, and teachers attended together. When these processes
take hold in a community, expensive due process hearings are not common.
The communities in Connecticut, like Hamden, Norwalk, and Manchester, that
utilized social workers in training school personnel in communication and
decision-making skills were much further ahead in parent-school positive
relations. Teachers and parents often think of themselves as the least
powerful. It is incumbent upon the profession of social work to change
that equation.

If teachers are not a part of the decision making, it will literally
come back and haunt a school system at a hearing. Teachers unable to articulate programs cannot be good witnesses. Teachers who are not listened
to will find other channels for their tales. If one is only thinking to
protect oneself, studies galore illustrate that the unhappy employee is in-
effective. When the teacher has an investment in the decision, energy is
released positively instead of negatively. A relatively frequent problem
in due process cases is a disgruntled teacher. They reach parents in a negative way. School social workers should be assigned to help with a positive
inclusion of teachers.

POWER AND "TURF"

Another significant factor that leads to unnecessary adversarial situations
is the whole arena of turf. This, too, is emphasized because of bureaucrat-
ic power plays. Understanding systems and what is happening when individuals act or fail to act or fail to act or speak is necessary information.
The infighting that takes energy and uses people's time can be almost crim-
inal. The methods that some personnel will use to be present at a team
meeting even when they do not know the child really should be attacked. Social work's contribution to group processes and team production is tremendous. 6/ Frequently the team member who feels threatened or insecure will
be the weak link either in not producing or projecting negative influences
on other team members or the parents. In a very affluent community during
a mediation, a pupil personnel staff member who was angry with the principal would not agree to a less restrictive setting for the child, although
the parents were requesting it. She held out in reality because she was
angry over not being given the final say in diagnosis. How decisions are
made, who has the power, how it is used are all questions that need to be
more openly discussed. School social workers can help set a more productive atmosphere within a school just as they do within a family. Much of
their knowledge and skill is transferable from family practice to the power
and turf problems within the school setting. One method to illustrate time
spent on turf struggles is to use the observer's assessment that the author
designed   for team decision making. The following are examples from the
assimilation phase:

1. What statements did anyone make that indicated fairness and open-
   mindedness?

42

2. What nonverbal approaches were made that indicated concern and appreciation of members of the group?

    a. Sitting between any antagonists.
    b. Bodily leaning toward anyone.
    c. Focusing eyes on speaker.
    d. Looking around group to include all who wanted to talk.
    e. By gestures, and eyes indicating total attention.

3. Did anyone refocus the different opinions in order to focus on the child's needs and program?

4. Did the focus on the child reduce the antagonisms, adversarial positions, misunderstandings or posturing? Yes _____ No _____ Which _____?

5. Did anyone assuage either side? Who? How?

6. Did anyone remain neutral? How was this demonstrated?

7. Did either side ramble or talk at length? Who cut through excessive verbalization? Was this used to try and wear the others down or was it due to the inability to focus on the problem?

8. Was all the written material displayed openly? Had it all been shown previously? Were there any misunderstandings over data? Were there any surprises?

9. What statements were made that clarified the essential factors and issues? Who made them?

10. What attitudes or statements indicated acceptance of school staff by parents? By parents of school personnel?

11. Were there any split opinions by staff members? How did this come about? Was it revealed to parents?

12. Who seemed to be more understanding of parents' problems?

13. Was anyone more concerned over the student? Who? Did this person understand the parents' position? Illustrate.

Further processes to evaluate if nonagreement is the outcome are vital for understanding, clarification, and team growth.

1. What ideas kept the sides apart?

2. What personality factors interfered with an agreement?

3. What legal aspects caused problems?

4. Who missed opportunities for obtaining agreement? Give opinion of why.

5. Which aspect of the session, personality, financial or legal, was the predominating reason for failure?

6. Was there a lack of trust? By whom?

7. Did the competitive nature of any individual cause the failure?

8. What aspects of federal or state or local laws or regulations worked against agreement? Which and why?

9. Did anyone from the school system talk down to the parents?

10. Was anyone from the school staff understanding of the parents' position? Not understanding? Who, in both instances.

11. Was anyone able to synpathize or identify with the parents' grief and concern over their child's handicapping condition?

12. What intra-turf problems caused the team problems?

13. What community implications hindered an agreement; that is, placement facilities, child guidance clinic, recreational programs, health-related agencies?

14. How was No. 13 addressed?

Another technique to follow is to chart the time taken for various stages. For example, noting the number of times the various members talk, for how long, who questions, who clarifies, who blocks, who is the facilitator, who is the supporter of the school program, are all aspects to assess. Videotaping team meetings and self-evaluating the session can be useful. In one training session, a guidance counselor questioned the author's procedure of receiving no information prior to the mediation. In role playing, she played the mediator, and in questioning wrote all the answers down in detail. On viewing herself on videotape, she was able to see herself distancing from the parents by her method. The trainer did not have to say anything, as the tape clearly demonstrated why a solution was not forthcoming. In the trainer's experience, one should only use tapes in training sessions, as a "chill" could be placed on the process in a real session.

Certain school procedures should be put into place in order to lessen the need for adversarial situations to erupt. Administrators who have utilized the full potential of their social work staffs in the author's opinion as a mediator and hearing officer have fewer unnecessary due process procedures. There will always be a number of difficult cases that either from a factual or emotional aspect could not be prevented. However, any special education director who does not assign problem areas to the school social work department is missing a step in prevention. Early referral should be made of fragile or vulnerable family conditions. In this way parents can very early have the option of meeting a helpful, nonblaming school representative. Where a positive helping tone is established, angry school personnel do not condemn parents who pursue their rights.

There are also people who really enjoy adversarial positions. We live in a litigious age, and parents are often encouraged to engage in legal battles. Once the adversarial process is started, some personality needs are met. It would be wise if any such individuals exist in a system to attempt to service them early before the anger and hostility take over. In the utilization of the caucus method, as a mediator one can often observe an abusive process, and by separating the parties, can thereby ameliorate the situation. It is necessary to focus on the needs of the child, taking it out of the struggle among the adults. In an extremely heated session, when the mother and chief administrator were screaming at each other, the student whispered to the mediator that he wanted to return to school. The mediator was able to capture the attention of the adults and repeat the boy's words. The adults then settled down and an agreement was reached. Early intervention by the school social worker at both ends of the spectrum of sensitive fragile families to bombastic fighting ones is recommended. All state departments of education have stories regarding hours spent on one case, usually of angry parents who were either ignored, dismissed, or not taken seriously enough.

LETTER WRITING

Another practice where school personnel need assistance is in the writing of letters and minutes of meetings. These should be evaluated in terms of the impact or meaning to the person receiving the letter. Many parents have confided to the author that they would never have gone to a hearing if the school had not written such a sarcastic letter or double-meaning minutes. In reviewing such written data, one is struck by the insensitivity of some personnel. School social workers should sensitize other staff members to parents' feelings in this area. Ambiguous statements or sarcastic phrases are another troubled area where blaming takes place. Training in phone techniques is an easy skill to teach.

School personnel need to be helped to deal with their feelings when they are criticized or in vulnerable shape themselves. They need assistance to understand their own frailties. However, the reinforcement of negatives by staff with each other is not helpful. In a mediation session in a small country town that had little experience with learning disabilities, a very well-meaning staff and principal had become hostile to a demanding parent. In the mediation, the mediator was able to show through the use of diagnostic material that the child's problem was serious and would not go away if the mother became less demanding. The school staff were really nice people but the mother had antagonized them so much that their wisdom was clouded. In another in-service session run by the author, several from that school attended. They all stated that an objective third person helped them refocus on the child and his program needs.

Another high priority recommendation is to assign school social workers to mediation and conciliation activities. There must be sanction from top administration if one assumes this responsibility. Many mediating tasks are accomplished by school social workers. Schwartz has advocated this role for school social workers for years. 7/ However, if one is assigned this role as a part of due process when contracts and agreements are in order, various other skills are required, as indicated previously in this article. School social workers have a natural proclivity for mediation processes. However, to maintain a presence in this role requires constant interpretation. Any role that is looked upon as powerful, which "due process" implies, is coveted. In addition, at the workshops sponsored by the grant-training mediators, other school professionals ardently desire the training. They are frequently put in the role of defending programs to parents and know how uncomfortable they feel in tense situations. Although it is vital to have all school personnel more open and impartial, school social workers are able to handle angry feelings, depressed individuals, and complicated interpersonal relationships more adroitly than most. Consequently, from just a time-factor point of view, this is an assignment particularly adapted for social work skill.

The relationships with community agencies is a natural linkage for professional school social workers. It is another space where cases fall between the cracks or turf problems evolve. Because P.L. 94-142 has appeal procedures established, many requests for due process are made that probably should be confined to other than educational agencies. In the category of the emotionally distressed, many difficult decisions have to be made. In one middle-sized city, a law school clinic brought charges of failure to educate a 17-year-old student. The school system had never heard of the student, as he was in a mental health facility. He had been sent to that facility from a school for the retarded. The law school clinic was correct to pursue the case, as there were no grounds for action other than under P.L. 94-142. Good school social work interagency planning was brought into play by the mediator and the two agencies jointly planned a program.

Often when interagency planning becomes significant, social workers are bypassed. Administrators want to keep the power and action for themselves. As this is so much a part of the expertise and milieu of the social work profession, educational administration would be wise to utilize and retain social workers in that role. Such workers can be of service to their clients and the community by establishing smooth working liaisons. There is often a tendency (even by social workers) to look at other agencies as the enemy. This attitude should be dispelled, as it is nonproductive. School social workers, more than anyone else in the educational agency, must bring a balance to community participation. Schools can become and have been islands. The social worker's goal should be to broaden and facilitate communication and participation throughout the human service network.

Many criticisms have been made of schools as well as social workers in this past decade. The 1980s are focusing on economic factors. Social work is identified with the world's ills. Previously, educators could dismiss their responsibility but not any longer. Every newspaper and radio station discusses "the failure of the schools to educate," and lawsuits are constantly being filed. This would be an excellent time to articulate the high quality of service that school social work can offer, especially in the painful area of parental criticism and legal cases. Social workers can demonstrate by early intervention, parent groups, changing attitudes, fewer turf struggles, better communications, and mediation assignments, that schools can be a productive place to learn and work. The profession of social work must document its procedures and learn to pronounce its successes. As our institutions become bleak, a ray of light looks like the sun at times. School social workers must capture the light and use the energy to change schools into warm, exciting learning institutions.

NOTES AND REFERENCES

1. See Arthur P. Michals, David E. Cournoyer, and Elizabeth L. Pinner, "School Social Work and Educational Goals," Social Work 24 (March 1979), pp. 138-141; and Jean F. Campbell, "Does Social Work Make a Difference?" Social Work in Education 1 (October 1978), pp. 4-18.

2. Jean Campbell, "Individualized Educational Programs as a Tool in Evaluation," Social Work in Education 2 (April 1980), pp. 19-24.

3. A. Solnit and M. Stark, "Mourning and the Birth of a Defective Child," Psychoanalytic Study of the Child, Vol. 16 (New York: International-al Universities Press, 1961).

4. Shirley L. Patterson, "The Grief Model: Applications Within the School," Social Work in Education 1 (October 1978).

5. Frank F. Maple, Shared Decision Making, Vol. 4 (Beverly Hills, Calif.: Sage Publications, 1977).

6. See. for example, Lawrence Schulman, Skills of Helping Individuals and Groups, (Itasca, Ill.: F.E. Peacock Publishers, 1979); and William Schwartz, "Between Client and System: The Mediating Function," in Robert W. Roberts and Helen Northern, eds. Theories of Social Work With Groups (New York: Columbia University Press, 1961).

7. Schwartz, op. cit.

SECURING AND UPGRADING
STATE CERTIFICATION:
AN OVERVIEW

E. VIRGINIA LAPHAM

In April of 1980, the National Association of Social Workers (NASW) Provisional Council on Social Work Services in Schools under the leadership of Anne Mitchell, applied to the Program Advancement Fund Committee of NASW for a special project grant relating to securing and upgrading state certification of school social workers.

Entitled "Achieving School System and State Department of Education Recognition of Professional Social Work," the threefold general purpose of the grant was (1) to explore specialty interest groups as a mechanism for the improvement of practice in specialty groups, (2) to promote public recognition and sanction of social work as a profession, and (3) to promote the direct involvement of social workers in the political process in order to impact governmental/public policy decision making.

The project was based in part on a doctoral dissertation by Hawkins. 1/ This study of state certification standards for school social workers revealed that a wide range of job titles and training and experience levels were recognized by states for use of the school social work title and for the provision of social work services in schools. For example:

> In one state, a professional social worker with an MSW must work as a visiting counselor and the visiting counselor position may also be filled by a person with two years classroom teaching experience with no social work training.

> In another state, MSW professional social workers must earn twenty-four credits in education and then take a teacher's licensing exam.

> In some states, certification is denied social workers.

In July of 1980, the project was approved and the Provisional Council on Social Work Services in Schools, then under the leadership of Lorraine Davis, had until June 30, 1981, to carry out the project. Molly Freeman, NASW School Social Work Coordinator, was given the staff responsibility for carrying out the project. On September 1, 1980, this author was hired as a consultant to work with the project under the supervision of Molly Freeman.

The tangible and measurable objectives of the project were listed as:

1. To identify a working leadership in five pilot states.

2. To work with each state group to develop a list of measurable objectives relevant to that state.

3. To identify those portions of the NASW standards for social work services in schools relevant to state certification.

4. In consultation with individual states, to identify and secure the services of an appropriate consultant.

5. To contact the National Education Association and the National Council on Accreditation of Teacher Education toward securing the adoption of NASW standards.

6. To prepare a state level work plan on progress and implementation.

7. To develop and produce a brochure on the state certification process.

The first step then was to make initial contacts with school social work leaders in five states that had previously contacted national NASW regarding interest in having some sort of assistance with certification problems in their respective states to determine their interest in participating in the project. Affirmative answers were received from contacts in Oklahoma, Ohio, Nebraska, New Mexico, and West Virginia. Copies of the grant were then sent to the contacts to be discussed with other interested social workers in the state in order to decide what specific objectives they would work on that year toward the overall goal of securing or implementing state certification. State NASW leaders were also contacted regarding the project. They were also requested to begin thinking about the kind of consultant that would be helpful to them, some specific names of consultants if they desired, and dates for use of the consultant.

SEEKING INFORMATION

While the five pilot states were determining their objectives and use of a consultant, the NASW staff coordinators of the project were consulting with other NASW national staff members for background information in the whole area of licensure and for input into the project generally; and contacting social work leaders in approximately fifteen other states regarding their experiences with state certification of school social workers. The questions asked were: What are the issues regarding certification of school social workers? What are the major concerns? Who are the key people to contact? and What are the snags in the process and how can they be avoided?

It was possible from this sample to synthesize some commonalities of issues, learn of unique situations, and have knowledge of both process and specific experiences to pass along to the five pilot states.

By early December 1980, the state of Nebraska leadership decided to withdraw from the project because of changed circumstances and lack of leadership to work on the project. School social work leaders in the state of Virginia had just begun experiencing problems with proposed changes in their certification for which they were requesting assistance, so Virginia became the fifth state in the project, replacing Nebraska.

In March 1981, the midyear project summary submitted by the now fully recognized NASW Practice Advancement Council on Social Work Services in Schools showed measurable objectives identified in four of the five states and consultants identified and scheduled for three of the states.

A draft of the proposed brochure was completed in April and mailed to all of the original consultants plus some national NASW staff members plus members of the NASW Practice Advancement Council on Social Work Services in Schools. This draft was also circulated at the 2nd National NASW Conference on School Social Work in May 1981 in order to have as many comments and suggestions as possible before writing the final brochure, which was to be made available to all of the states.

As of May 1981, all five of the pilot states had their objectives set, and consultants identified for meetings or conferences to be held prior to the end of June when the project was to end. The five consultants, all well known and highly qualified leaders in the field of school social work were:

1. Betty Welsh, Professor at Wayne State University in Detroit, who had already spent two days providing consultation and speaking at the state NASW conference in Oklahoma.

2. Marilyn Mabry, Consultant in Social Work with the state of Indiana, who would be going to Ohio later.

3. Lorraine Davis, State Social Work Consultant in Wisconsin, who would be providing consultation to social workers in New Mexico.

4. Lela Costin, Professor of Social Work, University of Illinois at Urbana-Champaign, who would be the consultant for Virginia social workers.

5. Betty Deshler, Associate Professor, Western Michigan University School of Social Work, who was scheduled to consult with the West Virginia Social Work leaders.

The only other component of the project was the presentation made at the Second National NASW Conference on School Social Work. The presentation had two purposes. One was to give social workers the opportunity to hear firsthand from: (1) Steve Montoya and Loretta Lopez, leaders in one of the grant states regarding the current issues and problems there; (2) Joan Harris, a leader in one of the states providing consultation to the project regarding her experiences in certification; and (3) Nancy Banchy, a leader who submitted a proposal for discussing certification in her state and was included on the panel because of the wealth of information it provided. The second purpose of the conference workshop was to allow participants to discuss experiences they have had regarding certification or to ask questions on which they seek group wisdom. The papers presented by Montoya and Lopez, Harris, and Banchy follow this overview.

NOTES AND REFERENCES

1. Mable T. Emanuel Hawkins, "State Standards for Certificated School Social Worker, Visiting Teacher, Attendance Worker, and Home-School Visitor," Publication No. 79-24, 716; School: University of Pittsburgh; Dissertation Abstracts International (Ann Arbor: Mich.: University Micro-films International, 1979).

EFFORTS TO UPGRADE SCHOOL
SOCIAL WORK CERTIFICATION
IN NEW MEXICO

Steve L. Montoya and Loretta Lopez

School social workers are certified in New Mexico by the State Department of Education. This article will go into a description of that certification (see Appendix 1), but will begin by giving a brief summary of the history of school social work in the state.

School social work in New Mexico has a short and somewhat turbulent history. In 1967, Roswell, a southeastern school district, used Title I money to hire an MSW. She was employed until 1972 when the district decided it did not want to continue to use Title I funds to provide such services. In an interview, this worker related how certain members of the community saw her as a welfare worker. They did not feel that a school system should be helping students and parents with welfare. She had to change her title to something other than school social worker for the short time she did work in this school system. Also around 1967, the Taos school district in northern New Mexico utilized the services of an MSW, who was actually employed by a local agency. In 1972, the Albuquerque public school district contracted for Title IV-A money (the predecessor of Title XX) to hire social workers. In 1973, the Santa Fe (state capital) district also contracted for social workers. Both districts continue to provide school social work services, although there have been some changes in funding sources. Currently, in the Albuquerque district there are ten school social workers and a program director. Five of the workers are funded under Title I and five are under special education funding through the state. New Mexico is the only state in the United States that does not utilize P.L. 94-142 money.

Even though New Mexico does not accept P.L. 94-142 funding, special education in the state is governed by state and federal laws and regulations. Basically, Section 504 of the Rehabilitation Act of 1973 (P.L. 93-112) regulations are followed by the state in providing special education. The five school social workers employed in 1981 by the Albuquerque district under special education came out of a district plan that was accepted by a federal judge. Several parent groups and associations dealing with handicapped children had filed court action against the state for not accepting P.L. 94-142. The state of New Mexico filed an appeal of the federal courts ruling that the state discriminates against handicapped children by not providing them an appropriate educational opportunity. The federal judge had ordered New Mexico to adopt the plaintiffs' plan for correcting deficiencies in special education in New Mexico. The Denver appeals court allowed a postponement of that order until the appeal was heard. As of 1981, this suit had been in progress for six years. The Albuquerque public schools plan, which included the hiring of social workers, was accepted by the federal judge. Also, during the 1980-81 school year, six other school districts each had a person designated as a school social worker. These districts were: Dulce, Española, Gallup-McKinley County, Taos, and West Las Vegas. In addition, the Las Cruces school district utilized undergraduate social work students. It also seemed that two private Indian schools, one in Santa Fe and the other near Grants, utilized a couple of MSWs. Most school districts in the state employed MSWs or BSWs as school social workers. However, there were three or four persons employed as school social workers who did not have social work degrees. In 1981, the authors were able to identify approximately twenty-five school social workers as being currently employed in the state.

The services provided by the school social worker are diverse, and the type and number of students receiving services is dependent on the funding source. In Albuquerque they are primarily Title I students, low-income students, or special education students. In general, the primary services provided by the school social workers include direct intervention with students and parents; outreach and liaison between schools, home, and community; staff consultation and development; and interdisciplinary collaboration and teaming with other pupil personnel specialists. Some districts have placed greater emphasis on one area of service than on another area. In Albuquerque, for instance, the emphasis is on working with parents to resolve family and/or environmental problems which make it difficult for students to function successfully in school.

EFFORTS TO OBTAIN STATE SUPPORT

In 1981, in the first session of the state legislature an effort was made to pass a bill to implement a statewide school social work program in school districts. House Bill 361 was introduced as the result of the work of the Juvenile Code Task Force on the childrens' code (see Appendix 2). The task force was formed as the result of a House Memorial, passed during the 1979 legislative session. The memorial was a compromise between legislators wanting to have an emphasis on prevention and rehabilitation and those legislators wanting a code with a more restrictive and tougher tone. The task force was chaired by a state representative in agreement with the former stance. Its vice-chairman was a state senator advocating the latter. The task force held public hearings throughout the state. Through this process certain gaps in services became apparent and the task force made program recommendations to begin to correct these gaps. A state funded school social work program received top priority among their recommendations.

Opposition to HB 361 came from persons opposed to the treatment over punishment orientation favored by the task force and persons who felt it was inappropriate for school districts to deal with social problems. The State Department of Education opposed the bill partially for the latter reason. Their primary opposition however, was based on their belief that the proposal was inconsistent with the intent of the equalization formula, which seeks to provide a uniform base of financial resources to all school districts, leaving the final decisions regarding how funds are spent to local boards of education.

The equalization formula utilizes cost differentials to reflect higher costs incurred in providing certain educational programs in order that the individual needs of students are met. The formula encourages local initiative through decategorization of fund usage and the absence of any fund "tracking system." Funding for each educational program is determined by calculating program units. Program units are calculated by multiplying the number of students in a particular program (or by multiplying programs as in the case of some special education programs) by the appropriate cost differential. (For example, the cost differential for some programs are: early childhood education = 1.3; grades 7-12 = 1.25; ancillary special education programs = 20.) The program units subtotal is then multiplied by the Educational and Training Index of that district. The formula also provides additional program units to reflect school size adjustment which primarily favors small, rural districts. The formula does not include cost differentials for support services such as counseling, nursing, or social work. Each school district must provide for such services, as they are mandated by state minimum standards (school social work is not mandated by the state) within their operational budget. The formula is as fair as can be since it guarantees 95 percent state funding to each district.

The children's code changes being recommended by the task force were not strongly supported. In working out a compromise to include some of the task force amendments, the school social work bill was sacrificed. It seems that the State Department of Education's concern that the bill would be seen by conservative legislators as a way of going around the equalization formula for additional funds for school districts was an effective argument.

In the future school social workers in New Mexico will work toward further growth and visibility of programs. They hope to bring up the state school social work bill again in some form. 1/ This may be fostered by the passing of House Memorial 42. The memorial requests that the Legislative Education Study Committee study the effects of social problems on school achievement and possible intervention strategies. As a state that was included in the NASW practice advancement grant on "achieving school system and state department of education recognition of professional social work," New Mexico was to be visited by Lorraine Davis, Chairperson of the Practice Advancement Council on Social Services in Schools, who was to consult with school social workers and the State Department of Education on the importance of having a consultant on school social work at the state level. The state's school social workers hope to continue efforts at impacting the State Department of Education and school districts on the importance of school social work as a needed resource to school districts.

NOTES AND REFERENCES

1. Among those involved in efforts to obtain state funding are: the present authors; Rosemary Sciame, Coordinator, Juvenile Code Task Force; Pam Najdowski, School Social Work Coordinator, Santa Fe Public Schools; Gerald Ortiz y Pino, Director, New Mexico Youth Work Alliance; and Michael McGarrity, past Coordinator, Santa Fe School Social Work Program.

Appendix 1. Department of Education, Santa Fe, New Mexico, Requirements for School Social Work Certification

All School Social Worker Certificates are issued by the New Mexico State Department of Education. Applicants must request their college to forward official transcripts of all college credit to: Teacher Education and Certification Unit, State Department of Education, Santa Fe, New Mexico 87503.

Five Year School Social Worker Certificate

I. Educational Requirements

   A. Bachelor's or Master's Degree in Social Work from a college or university regionally accredited or approved by the New Mexico State Board of Education.

   B. Evidence of eight (8) semester hours of appropriate credit earned within the five year period immediately preceding the date of application.

II. Experience Requirements

   A. One year of paid school social work experience during the five year period immediately preceding the date of application.

   B. Letter from employing school district certifying year(s) of paid work experience.

III. Renewal Requirements

   A. The Five Year School Social Worker Certificate may be renewed for five years at a time provided the holder earns eight (8) semester hours of credit during the five year period immediately preceding the date of application for renewal. Credit should be applicable toward meeting requirements for the Ten Year Professional School Social Worker Certificate or have the prior approval of the individual's employing authority or the Director of Teacher Education and Certification, New Mexico State Department of Education.

   B. Four (4) semester hours of inservice credit may be applied toward renewal. All renewal credit earned through inservice must be

55

approved by the employing authority and the Director of Teacher Education and Certification , New Mexico State Department of Education.

C. Letter from employing school district certifying year(s) of paid working experience.

Ten Year Professional School Social Worker Certificate

I. Educational Requirements

A. Master's Degree in Social Work from a college or university regionally accredited or approved by the New Mexico State Board of Education.

B. Evidence of eight (8) semester hours of appropriate credit earned within the five year period immediately preceding the date of application.

II. Experience Requirements

A. Three years of paid school social work experience during the five year period immediately preceding the date of application.

B. Letter from employing school district certifying year(s) of paid work experience.

III. Renewal Requirements

A. The Ten Year School Social Worker Certificate may be renewed for ten years at a time provided the holder earns eight (8) semester hours of credit during the ten year period immediately preceding the date of application for renewal. Credit should have the prior approval of the individual's employing authority or the Director of Teacher Education and Certification, New Mexico State Department of Education.

B. Four (4) semester hours of inservice credit may be applied toward renewal. All renewal credit earned through inservice must be approved by the employing authority and the Director of Teacher Education and Certification, New Mexico State Department of Education.

C. Letter from employing school district certifying five years of paid working experience within the last ten years.

One Year School Social Worker Certificate

The One Year School Social Worker Certificate will be issued to those persons meeting educational requirements for the Five Year School Social Worker Certificate but who have not had one year of paid school social work experience during the previous five year period.

The One Year School Social Worker Certificate will be issued by the State Certification Officer only upon the written request of a local school district.

Appendix 2. House Bill 361, Thirty-Fifth Legislature, State of New Mexico, First Session, 1981, an Act Making an Appropriation to the Department of Finance and Administration to Implement School Social Work Programs;

Declaring an Emergency a/

BE IT ENACTED BY THE LEGISLATURE OF THE STATE OF NEW MEXICO:

Section 1. APPROPRIATION.--One million five hundred thousand dollars ($1,500,000) is appropriated from the general fund to the public school finance division of the department of finance and administration for expenditure in the sixty-ninth and seventieth fiscal years for the purpose of implementing, coordinating, evaluating and maintaining a school social work program for the prevention and reduction of anti-social behavior. Such funds shall be distributed to local school districts for the purpose of employing school social workers. The public school finance division and the state board of education shall jointly promulgate rules and regulations establishing procedures and criteria for applying, qualifying and distributing funds from this appropriation and to provide guidelines for the implementing, coordinating, evaluating and maintaining services under the school social work program. Any unexpended or unencumbered balance at the end of the seventieth fiscal year shall revert to the general fund.

Section 2. EMERGENCY.--It is necessary for the public peace, health and safety that this act take effect immediately.

---

a/ This bill was patterned after the original written proposal submitted to the Juvenile Code Task Force by John Myers, Social Work Department, New Mexico State University, Las Cruces.

SOME PERSPECTIVES ON STATE
DEPARTMENT OF EDUCATION CERTIFICATION
OF SCHOOL SOCIAL WORKERS

JOAN Y. SEMBLY HARRIS

Those who advocate for certification for school social workers begin usually with certain basic assumptions: (1) that this is a desirable direction to take professionally, according to some set of values, (2) that certification is desirable for students and school systems according to some set of values and (3) that school social workers need to convince others of the desirability of their goal of certification so that it can be granted to them. Somehow, such seemingly simple understandings do not translate into the ends the profession seeks. There seem to be innumerable obstacles to overcome. What is self-evident to the profession about the rightness of its efforts eludes "the powers that be," and school practitioners are perplexed. It is for this reason that they come together in national conferences and that they hold state committee meetings--to try to understand why this is so difficult a task--achieving what the profession considers to be a desirable certification statute on the law books in all states. More than understanding, school social workers seek answers--strategies, approaches, and techniques to facilitate the accomplishment of their goals.

This article has two primary purposes, which present a paradox: (1) to briefly present a perspective on certification efforts that may prove helpful in influencing change and enhancing the prospects of achieving certification, and (2) to present a brief summary of the certification effort in Maryland, which effort has an assurance of success, for reasons unrelated to the perspective that will be shared.

As previously indicated, according to one set of values, school social work certification is a desirable goal. But what are the intended outcomes or the consequences of certification--what is it that the profession wants to occur as the result of certification? More and better services to students because more social workers will be delivering them? If this is what is wanted, will certification achieve this? Will certification per se translate into the outcome of effective services to students and more school social workers? It seems to the author that there are some process teps between the achievement of certification and the attainment of better and more effective services that might then lead to more school social workers being hired.

School social workers normally feel pretty comfortable with the idea

that social work services are valuable, desirable, and worthwhile, and
studies have been conducted that show improved achievement, attendance,
and behavior have resulted when social workers in schools have intervened.
Far too many in the profession have not materially demonstrated this within
their local systems. The result of this may be that while the mind-set
of school practitioners is clearly favorable towards their involvement,
those who make the final decisions about school social work certification
and those in school systems who must support social work efforts are not
as clear. To some of them certification per se may not be equated with
better services for students. However, if there is information clearly
showing how school social work services already in existence in a locality
have impacted favorably upon students and schools, and the profession uses
this information as part of its process of seeking certification or changes
in the certification laws, school social work's intended outcomes may be
clearer and more understandable to those who normally might oppose certification efforts. To put it differently, a statement that certification equals
improved and better services is not defensible. A statement that social
work programs have proved effective and thus justify the provision of such
services in more schools, and that certification can help accomplish this
may be more effective. It will not ensure the desirable outcome of more
services in schools, without another process occurring.

All of this is to point out several questions that should be considered
as the profession works toward certification: Is certification the real
goal or ultimate outcome school social workers want, or is it the means to
the outcome or goal they seek? Should there not be something about the
means or process undertaken that justifies the end? If this is true, what
are the implications for certification-seeking efforts?

Do practitioners not need clarity about their function as school social
workers, proof of their successes in supporting school system goals, and a
firm basis for stating the real outcomes that might be anticipated if the
profession hopes to convince state departments of education that there should
be certification?

Another factor relating to school system reactions to change has relevance
for change efforts in some states. It is a change effort because workers
are saying when they seek certification that the existing regularity is not
desirable or sufficient in some way. The intended outcomes of the profession's
efforts will involve changing an existing regularity which may be defined
as normal (usual) behavior or action or set of circumstances. The effort
would involve bringing in social workers to do what has not been done before,
or what may have been accomplished by other people, who may be perceived to
be doing it quite adequately. Or it would involve asking for a different
set of standards to govern those who perform social work tasks.

Those who try to change the usual way of doing things--an existing
regularity--have to realize that it will have different significance for
each group involved in a particular setting--the teachers, principals, other
administrators, parents, and so forth. One consequence of this difference

in values and significance is that there will be groups that will feel obligated to obstruct, divert, or defeat the proposed change. Recognizing and dealing with this source of opposition is not a matter of choice, preference or personal esthetics. The chances of achieving intended outcomes become near zero when the sources of opposition are not faced, if only because it is tantamount to denial or avoidance of the reality of existing social forces and relationships in the particular setting. (The author is indebted in this discussion to the insightful work of Sarason, who has produced a most informative and knowledgeable discourse on the unique nature of the school culture from a social-psychological and a sympathetic viewpoint). 1/

EFFORTS IN MARYLAND

The issues raised in the preceding discussion have general applicability although they were not consciously an important aspect of school social workers' recent efforts to gain certification in Maryland because workers there were in a unique position. Due to several fortuitous factors, it was not necessary to convince the top state education officials of the need for certification. School social workers had the active assistance of the leadership in the office of state certification and accreditation and the support of the state leaders in pupil personnel. However, it was essential that the procedural aspect be followed exactly as outlined by the state department. This was done, but it is a lengthy process due to time limitations and other state education priorities and as of this writing, certification was still pending.

The primary issues in Maryland have revolved around problems related to the historical development of educational programs and services in the state. Baltimore City had until the last ten years more or less operated essentially as a separate entity in education, while the twenty-two counties operated under the aegis of the Maryland State Department of Education (MSDE). School social work evolved in Baltimore City from the introduction of the visiting teacher in 1938. It was apparently not until the 1960s that school social work services were instituted in other localities within the state. There are only fifty-six social workers under that title in Baltimore City schools and a total of seventy-two in the entire state. All have master's degrees. Montgomery County had the state's next largest contingent of school social workers--fifteen--but due to political manipulations within the system, was expected to have that number reduced to ten.

While school social work services developed in Baltimore City, the counties' support services included a professional group with teacher credentials entitled pupil personnel workers (PPWs) who performed tasks similar to school social workers. Pupil personnel workers have a consultant at the MSDE and a strong professional organization and they had successfully opposed social work certification for years. Eventually PPW certification criteria were revised in an unsuccessful effort to accommodate social workers who might wish to seek PPW certification, which is an alternative unacceptable to the school social workers.

The present author was not actively involved in previous efforts to secure certification. When she accepted a position with the Baltimore City Public Schools' Division of Pupil Services in November 1977, a certification proposal had been denied in June 1977. It appeared that previous efforts may have failed partially due to the lack of active internal school system support, particularly from the Baltimore City Public School administration, where the overwhelming majority of social workers were located. In the spring of 1978, the present author decided to include among her goals the reopening of the matter of school social work certification. Briefly, the initial process included personal conversations, and follow-up letters with MSDE Department of Pupil Personnel officials and a letter approved by the Baltimore City system's assistant superintendent of pupil personnel services to be sent under the signature of the superintendent of public instruction to the state superintendent of schools. This letter was a supportive one, detailing the integral role social workers play in Baltimore City schools in addressing the social, intellectual, emotional, and learning problems of children and adolescents. It also described specific programs in which school social workers were involved. It questioned the decision to deny certification and requested the basis for the decision, and so forth.

The state superintendent, who was relatively new in his position, had a legal background, which implied he had logical, orderly thought processes which it was hoped would be repelled by such a nonsensical situation. Also, he was not entrenched in county internal politics and loyalties. The result was that a positive process was begun, in which MSDE approval was promised. A representative committee of state school social workers was formed, with National Association of Social Workers representation; a simple draft was prepared listing a master's degree in school social work from an accredited school as the minimum requirement for certification. All state pupil personnel department heads and other affected or interested individuals and organizations reviewed and reacted to the proposal, and an activity log was maintained listing all actions, including meetings, and responses. This was important to show the extent of involvement of others in the proposal development stage and that due consideration had been given to everyone's response.

In summary, it is suggested that school social workers examine their expressed and unexpressed motives for seeking certification to determine if there is congruency (a fit) between their expressed goals and the means they undertake to accomplish them. It seems likely that the reasons that school social workers are seeking certification are professional recognition and enhancement. They realize this is an unacceptable argument for certification in most states, so they profess that certification will benefit students and schools. This is a concept that is not as clear and apparent to state boards of education as it is to school social workers. The author's experience in Maryland reinforces her belief that it is very hard for social workers to explain what they do so much differently (and perhaps better) than other professionals in schools that justifies developing another set of certification standards. School social workers have a difficult time demonstrating how they make a difference. So they need to build into their approach to certifi-

cation, mechanisms and activities that will facilitate reaching the goal of
certification as well as the ultimate goals of more services, once certification has been achieved. Certification processes might also proceed more
smoothly if social workers better understand the culture of schools and the
power of the existing regularity. A very basic question to ask ourselves
is, What do we expect certification to accomplish--and can it?

NOTES AND REFERENCES

1. See Seymour B. Sarason, The Culture of the School and the Problem
of Change (Boston: Allyn & Bacon, 1971), pp. 59 and 63.

ONE STATE'S EXPERIENCE:
UPGRADING STANDARDS

Nancy Kramer Banchy

The purpose of this paper is to describe one state's experience in securing licensure standards for social workers serving children and youth in the public schools. The experience spans thirty-three years, and a continuum of standards from stringent to generous to current compromise. Such fluctuation may appear erratic, to some in fact regressive. It is suggested, however, that the established social work dictum "begin where the client is" applies. Licensure standards cannot be considered apart from the conditions which characterize the state, the educational system, and the school social work program to which the regulation applies. As the conditions vary, so will licensure standards.

The paper has three components: a historical review of school social work and licensure in Minnesota; a summary of the current licensure proposal; and a discussion of the questions and issues addressed in developing it.

HISTORICAL REVIEW

The first school social work program in Minnesota was established in the Minneapolis Public Schools in 1917. Early responsibilities centered on attendance, but later expanded to include services to students with a broader spectrum of social and emotional problems. In 1948, certification standards--now termed licensure standards--were secured specifying one year of graduate training as mandatory for this growing group of "visiting teachers." Minnesota enacted legislation in 1957 making the delivery of special education services also mandatory, and soon thereafter school social workers were identified as "essential personnel" for whose employment local districts could be reimbursed by Special Education.

Such reinforcement had two predictable repercussions which ultimately affected licensure requirements: an increase in the number of districts employing school social workers, and an expansion of role functions. In 1962, a committee comprising representatives from higher education, the Minnesota State Department of Education, school social work practice, and regular education met to discuss whether standards "should be revised to a higher level." The proposal's rationale, not unfamiliar today, included: the need to protect the public and encourage optimal professional performance; and the official policy of the National Association of Social Workers (NASW), which was to "limit the use of the title 'social worker' to persons who have a master's degree in social work from an accredited school of social work." Although recognizing that social work was generic in nature, the committee also recognized "the necessity for an orientation to and knowledge of schools as a social institution." Their proposal, which was approved, therefore established the MSW with one year of fieldwork or work experience in a school setting as the basic criteria. A provisional certificate with additional experience or academic qualifications allowed the candidate to gain a year of school experience for a standard certificate.

Throughout the 1960s, Minnesota's standards were congruent with the national trend. In the 1976 national survey conducted by NASW, the large majority of school social workers held the master's degree, and most districts required graduate-level training. Once again, however, in 1969, state exigencies precipitated a review of licensure standards. Since many of these were also relevant in the debate surrounding the current proposal, they deserve examination.

Shift in Staffing Patterns

Reimbursement, and the expansion of mandated services to handicapped students, influenced the pattern of employment of school social workers. In 1965 it was estimated that only 17 school social workers were employed outside of the seven-county metropolitan area; gradually this number increased to the 1981 total of 153 social workers. The rising demand for school social work services outside of the metropolitan area was gratifying, but problematic in that graduate-trained workers and graduate training programs were concentrated in urban areas.

Critical Social Problems--1960s

The recognition of the critical social problems facing the society, the legislative and judicial efforts to address them, combined with the civil rights movement, created an increased demand for social work services in the schools--particularly in the two major urban centers in Minnesota. Suddenly, demand exceeded supply; recruitment in urban areas was also a problem.

Diversified Population Needs

With the flight-to-the-surburbs phenomenon and the influx of minority groups to the cities, schools in the urban centers were faced with meeting the varying educational needs of different economic and sociocultural groups. Schools needed to recruit workers representing these groups; standards, basically eliminating experience as a criterion, constricted the candidate pool during this period.

Changing School Social Work Goals and Methods

Societal changes brought renewed attention to the need for additional social work goals and methods in schools. Candidates for licensure with the necessary prerequisites were primarily trained to deliver casework services. Others, without the academic qualifications, had gained experience in working with the community and groups through agency employment. Some believed that innovation and change were diminished through limiting the candidate pool.

Professional Status

In 1969--the year a task force was meeting in Minnesota to develop new recommendations for licensure--NASW in effect established the bachelor's degree in social work as the educational requirement for the first level of professional social work practice by voting to admit workers with that degree to full membership in the organization. No doubt many of the same exigencies operating in Minnesota were among those which precipitated this momentous step in the social work profession. The factor, however, gave professional legitimacy to the licensure change about to be recommended in Minnesota.

In 1969, a task force, once again with a broad representation from the education and social work communities, recommended that two levels of licensure be established. Level II essentially maintained the previous licensure requirements: an MSW with one year of fieldwork or work experience in schools, or two years of other work experience. Level I, however, could be obtained by a candidate with a major or its equivalent in social work, sociology, psychology, or cultural anthropology, and two years of experience in a social service agency. A supervision requirement for renewal was included, but never monitored or enforced. The pool was now wide open, the results of the "overflow" soon to be discovered.

To their credit, the developers were not shortsighted. They included the following recommendations that could have prevented excesses:

1. A small committee would be appointed to aid in assessing candidates whose credentials might not be easily established under these rather vague standards. The committee was never established.

2. Each school system would be required to have available the services of a Level II (MSW) worker. Differentiated staffing would be promoted and supervision assured. No such requirement was ever enacted, although certainly many districts did employ workers licensed at both levels.

3. Supervision--one-half day per week--would be provided workers licensed at Level I. Supervision, until 1980, was not monitored in Minnesota.

The results of a realistic effort to adapt to changing societal conditions and educational needs can be briefly summarized. One major accomplishment: recruitment was no longer a problem. By the 1980-81 school year, approximately 400 school social workers were employed in what equaled 340 reimbursed full-time positions in Minnesota. In a 1979 count, approximately 38 percent of the workers were licensed at Level I, a two-to-one majority of these employed in outstate Minnesota. The majority of all school social workers in Minnesota have provided adequate, if not outstanding, services to children and families. The litany of hazards about to be recited is not meant to reflect upon the professionalism or integrity of most of these school social workers. There were manifold problems, however.

1. The status of school social work had been maligned. A familiar quip: "Anyone can get a social work license." Professionals serving in host settings share a common problem: their role is often not clearly defined or understood by their colleagues. This was exacerbated when candidates trained in vaguely related areas were licensed to serve in the role. The outcome: the notion that "anyone can get a license" extended to "anyone can do social work."

2. Individuals have been licensed as school social workers, and practiced as such, without having taken one academic course in social work. It was assumed that they had gained some knowledge, understandings, and abilities through the required two-year work experience, which was vaguely defined in the license as a "social work or social welfare position in a social agency." Substantiation of this through perusal of written job descriptions was difficult at best. At the least, it was doubtful that these candidates had a strong identification with the values and ethics of the profession--or the profession itself.

3. Within the past decade, school districts have begun to employ personnel to work in unlicensed specializations such as chemical dependency, human relations, and child care. The generous provisions of the Level I requirements were an alternative. The repercussions: An individual could gain seniority in a system as a school social worker without appropriate training, and--if layoffs became a reality--replace a fully credentialed, trained school social worker.

CURRENT LICENSURE PROPOSAL

While recognizing that the two levels of licensure, concomitant with federal and state special education legislation, significantly increased the number of districts employing school social workers, members of the Minnesota School Social Workers Association became alarmed about the effects of the questionable standards. Leaders in the discipline had always been the catalysts in seeking and gaining beneficial regulation; once again, in 1976, they began efforts which culminated in t'e submission of a proposal to the Minnesota Board of Teaching in January 1981. The timing was propitious: a recommendation had been made in 1979 by the Special Education Department to review and revise all special education licensure. The Board of Teaching--responsible for approval of licenses-- designated a fifteen-member task force to review licensure recommendations of the department, to solicit reactions from interested parties, and to make final recommendations. School social work licensure was included for revision, and now, in effect, had a mandate for review. Because the discipline had no state-level representation, the state organization was asked to adopt and present a draft to the Special Education Task Force. Two elements proved advantageous: the work of the committee in debating issues surrounding licensure since 1976; and creation of a school social work specialist position in the Department of Education in 1979. School social work was well prepared to present a proposal for approval. The following are outlines of the two draft proposals:

School Social Worker Level I

A. All candidates recommended for license shall (1) hold a bachelor's degree in social work (BSW), (2) satisfactorily complete skill requirements in special education, and (3) satisfactorily complete a Level I school social work preparation program, approved by the Minnesota Board of Teaching.

B. Each program leading to the licensure of Level I school social workers shall provide candidates with training in the following areas: (1) basic knowledge, understandings, and abilities in methods of social work intervention, consultation, collaboration, teaming, referral, psychosocial assessment, and evaluation, (2) observation of special education and regular education programs, and (3) fieldwork of 400 hours during one school year in a school setting under the supervision of a practicing School Social Worker II.

School Social Worker Level II.

A. All candidates recommended for license shall (1) hold a master's degree in social work (MSW), (2) satisfactorily complete core skill requirements in special education, and (3) satisfactorily complete a Level II school social work preparation program approved by the Minnesota Board of Teaching.

B. Each program leading to the licensure of Level II school social worker shall provide candidates with training in the following areas: (1) basic knowledge, understandings, and abilities in methods of social work intervention, consultation, collaboration, teaming, referral, psychosocial assessment, evaluation, and supervision, (2) observation of special and regular education programs, and (3) fieldwork of 480 hours during one school year in a school setting under the supervision of a practicing School Social Worker II. (May substitute one year of experience in a school social work position for this requirement.)

QUESTIONS AND ISSUES

In developing the current licensure proposal the following questions were addressed.

1. <u>What would be the implication in Minnesota of reverting to previous, higher standards that would be compatible with NASW recommendations for the MSW as the preferred degree for practice entry?</u> There has been a significant increase in social workers in outstate Minnesota since 1965 which has obviously created services for students and families in areas with few mental health resources. The trend in these districts has been to employ undergraduate workers (Level I), perhaps in part due to the unavailability of graduate trained workers in rural areas of Minnesota, and the limited opportunities for continuing graduate education while employed. Also contributing may have been the inability, or unwillingness, of districts to employ higher salaried personnel. Elimination of the Level I category would have significantly reduced services to children and families in those areas where the need was greatest. In addition, any possibility for the professional and cost-effective advantages accrued through differentiated staffing patterns would have been eliminated. Several special education cooperatives in outstate areas have employed a cadre of Level I workers supervised by a Level II worker--an effective delivery model.

2. <u>Can the two-level licensure model be structured to assure that quality school social work services would be delivered throughout the state?</u> There has been concern in Minnesota, as elsewhere, that escalating demands upon school social workers in recent years have increased the need for upgrading standards. The focus of practice has turned from individual casework toward more involvement with family, school, and community systems; consultation and planning with school and agency personnel; and policy and program development. Trends in society and its schools--mainstreaming, desegregation, family disorganization and dysfunction, and chemical abuse--have added to the complexities of the social work role. School social workers practice in a host setting, often isolated from others in their profession. Some have believed that only graduate training could adequately prepare them for these challenges.

To balance this concern, however, was the outcome of the accreditation of undergraduate BSW programs by the Council of Social Work Education. Minnesota has nine excellent undergraduate social work programs, most offering fieldwork placements in schools. A review of their curricula indicated that candidates could obtain the basic knowledge, understandings, and abilities necessary for effective social work practice. When licensure standards delineated academic credentials, and assured that candidates would obtain them through training programs approved on the basis of meeting established criteria, a basic safeguard was achieved. The second protection was the assurance of professional supervision. Although provision for professional supervision was not contained within the licensure standards, it was established in Minnesota's special education rules and had been monitored for compliance since 1980. It was the belief of the proposal developers that specificity of training and supervision in practice--assured through licensure and rules--could provide sufficient assurance of quality services, while allowing flexibility in employment and staffing patterns.

3. When there are separate licenses based on levels of training, are there also different expectations for the holder's role and function? This issue posed a dilemma. In practice, in Minnesota, and probably elsewhere as well, there was little differentiation by role between the MSW and BSW workers. A structured, differentiated staffing model was rare, and then differentiation was only on the basis of supervisory responsibility. One basic difference was regulated through special education rules: a Level I worker must have professional supervision by a Level II worker; the latter was able to practice independently.

Differentiation in the licensure was addressed in the delineation of knowledge, understanding, and abilities which approved training programs must provide candidates. In this context, "knowledge" means familiarity with and exposure to the subject area, relating theory to educational practice; and "ability" means demonstrated skill in the implementation of the subject area. In developing program categories, competencies necessary for social work practice in schools were designated, followed by identification of the knowledge and understanding pertinent for each. Differentiation was addressed in the following ways: The Level II candidates are most likely to have understanding (in-depth comprehension) of subject areas in the various categories. They are expected to have completed training programs with abilities to provide leadership and staff development programs; to participate in policy and program development; to understand and intervene in systems; and to use community organization skills. They are also expected to understand theories, styles, and strategies of supervision and to demonstrate abilities to transmit knowledge and foster skills.

In summary, the licensure proposal reflected the belief that both BSW and MSW workers were prepared for entry-level practice and to provide direct professional intervention with students and families, the BSW with professional supervision, the MSW independently. The MSW worker has been trained, in addition, to provide professional supervision, to assume leadership, training, and policymaking roles, and to intervene in systems. The proposal developers believed that sufficient differentiation existed to justify maintenance of the two-level model.

4. Should licensure standards for school social workers require training components specific to practice in school settings? Training programs for social workers have generally been generic. As school social work practice moved from traditional casework with individuals to more involvement in the total educational process, it had become apparent that new roles required new preparation. Generic training had not adequately prepared workers to further their host setting's goal--the education of children and youths. In addition, there was recognition that when workers practiced in host settings, there was need to establish and maintain credibility as a discipline. The question was too often asked: How can school social workers consult and advise when they have no experience in, or knowledge of, the field of education? These two forces--the changing goals of practice and the establishment of credibility

in a host setting--convinced the proposal developers that the license must reflect the unique needs of the practice setting. Knowledge, understandings, and abilities needed by candidates were established. Fieldwork experience relevant to practice in schools was specified. Core skill areas in special education--requirements for all of the licenses under review--were incorporated into the proposal.

5. <u>Should the licensure standards require work experience in addition to academic training and fieldwork?</u> There was no debate concerning work experience for Level II workers. Inasmuch, however, as this had been a strong element in the most recent license for Level I workers, and many believed it to be a necessary adjunct to a BSW degree, there was considerable deliberation. Probably no other issue created as much consternation among practitioners and employers of school social workers. Included in the original draft, the two-year requirement was seen by many as a deterrent to recruiting qualified candidates. With the new focus on specialization in academic training, and fieldwork in schools, it was feared that the school-related knowledge and experience gained would be lost in a two-year placement elsewhere. Candidates themselves might be lost to other specializations, particularly if districts were unwilling, or unable, to provide compensation for the two years of experience. Concomitantly, it was agreed that the strong social work educational and fieldwork requirements in the license diminished the need for work experience.

CONCLUSION

Since 1948, school social work in Minnesota has gained valuable experience in the area of licensure. A balance which met the needs of practitioners, the state's educational system, and the children and families to be served, has been difficult to achieve. The standards have always been developed by practitioners; they have been shaped, however, by the conditions and needs of the time--as they should be. It is believed that the proposed license--if approved in future months--addresses the exigencies of this time, while moving toward assurance of quality professional services. One certainty: School social workers will be meeting again within the decade to debate and revise licensure standards to meet the exigencies of that day.

DEVELOPMENTAL AND MAINTENANCE ISSUES OF
A UNIVERSITY-SPONSORED, STATE-APPROVED
SCHOOL SOCIAL WORK PREPARATION PROGRAM

Mable T. Emanuel Hawkins

Included in the many responsibilities of state departments of education are those related to pupil personnel services and the certification of school personnel of which school social workers have become a significant part. Institutions of higher education, therefore, as resources for training, are intrinsically involved in the development, implementation, and evaluation of preparation programs for certification of such personnel.

Ellis and Bryant in their article concerning competency-based certification indicated that there has been a shift in the method of evaluating professional social work practice "from that of accounting for process activities to that of accounting for practice outcomes." [1] According to Ellis and Bryant, some of the forces contributing to the move toward competency-based accreditation in reference to social work preparation include the difficulty in accounting for practice and its results in clearly definable outcomes, and the general thrust toward management and accountability procedures in industry, the government and other helping professions such as health and education. Social work preparation has been influenced further, under the leadership of the National Association of Social Workers (NASW) in establishing the Academy of Certified Social Workers (ACSW); through the encouragement of NASW for states to develop licensure procedures for social workers; and by the continuing engagement of state departments of education, institutions of higher education, local education agencies, and relevant professional associations in negotiations to establish competency-based education for school personnel. [2] Thus, shifting trends in the field of education relative to competency-based education, in addition to other societal factors, have had significant influence upon program accrediting procedures involving licensure and certification. These influences also have had an impact upon the degree to which university-sponsored, state-approved school social work programs have been initiated and maintained.

The purposes of this article are: (1) to identify some commonalities among special, state-mandated, school social work preparation programs; (2) to describe the developmental process of a specific university-sponsored, state-approved school social work certification program; (3) to identify for educational and practice purposes the dilemmas and complexities involved in attempting to enhance competency levels of school social work practitioners through university social work training programs when major controls for support of such preparation programs remain external to the university and professional social work educators and practitioners; and (4) to emphasize a critical need for closer collaboration among social work and education professionals at federal, state, and local levels for the provision and maintenance of high-quality social work services and expertise in school settings.

SOME COMMONALITIES

In Hawkins' study of state standards for certification of school social workers, it was indicated that forty-two, or 82.4 percent of fifty-one responding state departments of education reported certification of diverse school social work position titles. Further, this study revealed that the position title most frequently endorsed is "school social worker" by twenty-nine (69.5 percent) of the forty-two certificating states. 3/ Of the twenty-nine states endorsing the position title "school social worker," nine or 31 percent, reported requirements for completion of special school social work preparation programs for state certification. However, two of the nine responding states indicated alternatives to the special preparation program requirement for certification.

Of the forty-two certificating states, thirteen or 30.9 percent indicated endorsement of alternate position titles for certification of the school social work service personnel. Three or 23 percent of these thirteen responding states reported requirement of a special school social work preparation program. Again, two of the reporting three states indicated alternate routes for certification. 4/

Several commonalities, in training and experience areas, were noted in relation to the special preparation programs. First, the master of social work (MSW) degree was indicated as a requirement for certification by the total of twelve states stipulating special programs. Second, adherence to values of the profession; general knowledge of the school system and school laws; core knowledge and skills supportive of a generalist approach to intervention in school or school related problems; and a field experience in the school setting seemed to be common components in curriculum designs for the special preparation programs. 5/

In 1976, the University of Utah reported the results of a feasibility study for a career field specialization in social work in education. This study involved a request from the university for information regarding emphases in social work and education across the graduate schools of social work. Among the commonalities found in this study is an identified need and interest in research as part of the classroom and field experience for students in a school social work program. 6/

Other findings of the Utah study indicated cooperation be ween a number of schools of social work and education, several of which have developed certification programs to comply with state requirements. These universities include: Loyola University at Chicago, the University of Pittsburgh, Case Western Reserve University, the University of California at Berkeley, the University of Georgia, the University of Michigan, Ohio State University, the University of Washington at Seattle, and the University of Utah. 7/

UNIVERSITY OF PITTSBURGH PROGRAM

In Pittsburgh, Pennsylvania, between 1940 and 1952, early efforts were undertaken by two educators, Florence Poole and Jane Wille, to promote the professional status of school social work. These professors succeeded in establishing and maintaining cooperative working relationships between the University of Pittsburgh and the Pittsburgh Board of Education through the development of training programs for both the employed "home and school visitors" (position title endorsed by the Pennsylvania Department of Education for certification of school social workers) and the Graduate School of Social Work students. In addition to providing quality training for graduate interns the efforts of Poole and Wille helped to stimulate interest among the employed home and school visitors to seek professional social work preparation. 8/

Until 1969, state certification procedures for professional personnel to work in public schools involved satisfactory completion of the National Teachers Examination and transcript analysis. However, during that same time, the Commonwealth of Pennsylvania and other states across the nation were engaging in innovative approaches to the preparation and certification processes. The approved program approach, recommended by the Advisory Committee on Teacher Education to the State Council of Education on July 1, 1957, resulted in the initiation of program approval procedures by the Pennsylvania Department of Education during the 1962-1963 school year. Adoption of Pennsylvania Code, Title 22, Chapter 49--Certification of Professional Personnel reinforced the approved program approach effective July 1, 1969. 9/

The new set of regulations denoted a drastic departure from the type of regulations previously in effect. The most marked change occurred in the area of responsibility for certification. Previously this responsibility fell on the Bureau of Certification. The task of evaluation of credentials was now to reside with the preparing institution and operate through the mechanism of "Program Approval." 10/ Under the program approval approach to certification, a person who is a graduate of an approved program and who has been recommended by the college as having successfully demonstrated competency in the area of certification, automatically receives a certificate by the Superintendent of Public Instruction.

Program approval thus became the directing force which helped to determine the nature and content of the preparation program, and in effect set the certification standards. An ad hoc committee made up of key personnel including college educators in the program area, practitioners and administrators assisted the Bureaus of Teacher Certification and Pupil Personnel Services of the Department of Education in the development of guidelines for certification and program approval in school social work. 11/

Between 1965 and 1969, a small committee of Pitt faculty from Schools of Social Work and Education collaborated on developing an educational program at the postbaccalaureate level for home and school visitors.

Initial program approval was sought and granted by the Pennsylvania Department of Education in 1971 (pending an on-site visit in May, 1972). Consequently, the University of Pittsburgh School of Social Work and Education began the first jointly sponsored Home and School Visitor Certification Program in the State in the Fall of 1971. 12/

This pilot program had been established partially in response to a request from the State Department of Education to initiate a model certification program that other schools in the state might follow. It was based on behavioral competencies, rather than transcript review, which had been the basis for certification prior to the new state regulations. The Pittsburgh Board of Education was most desirous of this certification training, since not all of its fifty-eight employed Home and School Visitors during 1969-70 were certified. In many school districts Home and School Visitors and School Social Workers were being hired as substitute teachers because there were no approved certification programs to enable them to qualify for the Educational Specialist categories under the revised certification standards. Finally, MSW graduates who did not qualify for certification generally were not employed by school districts, since school districts were not reimbursed for any portion of salaries paid to noncertified professional personnel.

After the on-site visit by the Pennsylvania Department of Education on July 17-19, 1972, provisional approval of the twenty-four-credit-hour program was granted on February 8, 1973. The program was part time, extending over a five-term period, thus accommodating the certification needs of persons already working in school systems. The program also provided an opportunity for upward mobility in pursuance of professional education. Consequently, courses were offered after school hours as well as during the summer. At all levels of entry, programs were designed to fit individual student backgrounds. Certification students working in the schools were required to be supervised by school personnel with MSW training and Home and School Visitor certification.

The course work involved twenty-four credits; twelve credits in social work; nine credits in education; three credits in a seminar course, team taught by a social work faculty member and an education faculty member. Applicants were required to complete a field practicum (school field placement three days a week for one term under MSW supervision). All specified courses were offered at 4:30 p.m., early evening, or on Saturday.

Credits earned in the certification program could be applied to a master's degree in social work or education. In order to obtain such credits, the applicant would be required to apply for and be admitted to either degree program. Credits were applicable only within five years after course work was completed. However, admission to the certification program did not guarantee admission to the degree program. As a result of the diversity of student needs, including both degree and nondegree students, more options relative to course selection are offered in both the social work and education areas of curriculum. A council composed of representatives from several disciplines, including health, serves as a coordinating advisory body with responsibilities of providing philosophical and academic linkages to effect a sound home and school visitor (school social worker) preparation program.

DEVELOPMENTAL DILEMMAS

In attempting to implement the provisionally approved program, the University of Pittsburgh found itself in dilemmas arising from a lack of resources allocated for support of the program, and a dual situation so far as commonwealth certification practices in this particular area are concerned. In contrast to the twelve students who initially entered the program in 1971, there were fifty-four students in 1973 and 1974. 13/ This situation in relation to faculty was critical since the program coordinator in addition to a full teaching and advising load for regular MSW students, had sole responsibility for advising, registering, and consulting with all home and school visitor students and other interested persons. Daily inquiries and requests for admission to the program were continuing to come in from individuals living within and outside of Allegheny County.

Although the Advisory Council was in general agreement that the program objectives were educationally and philosophically sound, the more demanding issues for maintaining and implementing such a program centered around an economic question relative to how the Schools of Education and Social Work could provide additional needed faculty. The State Department of Education recommendation of joint appointments for program coordinators was inextricably related to the economic factor. 14/ In September, 1974, because of administering problems involving unresolved questions around continuing the program, and the excessive overload for the program coordinator, the Advisory Council agreed to a moratorium on new nondegree admissions until further study, review, and decisions by the University of Pittsburgh administrative body.

Another example of need for additional faculty arose in the effort to integrate field practicums among the programs of Schools of Education and Social Work. Coordination and implementation of these plans required greater faculty input than was available. Possible resources, to compensate for faculty work overload, were explored through review of the tuition accrued by student registrations, and through consultation with university administrations, but again sufficient funding seemed unavailable.

Reflected in the university's position on the question of allocating resources for the program was the factor of a steadily decreasing job market for home and school visitors-school social workers. This situation was also indicative of the national fiscal state and the trend to curtail certain social service and educational programs. Thus, an administrative review and decision regarding continuation of the program seemed indicated. Lacking allocated resources for implementing a part-time nondegree home and school visitor program, the Advisory Council proposed that the program become a subspecialty of the MSW degree program. The core curriculum would remain basically the same, with the Advisory Council continuing to serve as an interdisciplinary, integrating, and evaluating body. The proposal was agreed to by administrators of both the school of social work and the school of education.

By accepting for certification only persons who are seeking the MSW degree, there is the effect of preparing the individual much more extensively and intensively than is required by the state standards for home and school visitor (school social workers) certification. Nevertheless, this plan is congruent with the university and the school of social work direction towards maintaining the highest level of preparation programs for professional practice. Ginevan cites Pittsburgh's urban problems, such as crowded housing, changing neighborhoods, increasing crime rate, inner-city deterioration and subsequent loss of middle- and upper-class population and their tax money, as major issues affecting publicly perceived needs for the provision, extent, and quality of home and school visitor services. 15/

Teachers' strikes, in Pittsburgh (and many other cities across the nation) have resulted in financial constraints upon school district budgets. According to Shelton, "current and impending cutbacks in school budgets will almost certainly make the use of paraprofessionals in school social work even more attractive to administrators." 16/ This set of circumstances leads to consideration of another major cause of dilemmas confronting developers of school social work preparation programs. Namely, unclear identification by professional working title of the type of services to be performed by school personnel engaged in the provision of social services. There have been many regulations passed by the state of Pennsylvania giving a legal basis to the home and school visitor's title and role, but not to the professional school social work position. Sections of the School Laws of Pennsylvania, 1971, reveal an interchangeable legal authority and nomenclature for home and school visitor and attendance officer personnel.

Another signficiant factor which influences the establishment of effective school social work preparation programs is the necessary appointment of a professional social worker to the Pupil Personnel Division of the State Department of Education. The Pennsylvania State Education department in 1960, organized a department of pupil services, but the department did not appoint a professional representative for school social work (home-school visitor). In 1981, the position for a social work specialist continued to remain vacant, and with a freeze on hiring plus federal funding cuts, it was possible that this slot might not be filled for an indefinite period of time. The results were limited direction and organization for developing programs which would support the values of the social work profession and optimal use of professional social work skills in services to the schools.

Finally, a crucial situation exists in relationship to the current dual certification system for home and school visitors in Pennsylvania. Certification may be attained by transcript review process through the Division of Teacher Certification, by indefinite standards, in the State Department of Education or by completing an approved certification program such as the one which is sponsored by the School of Social Work, University of Pittsburgh.

The University of Pittsburgh's achievement of five-year program approval
in 1975, by the State Department of Education for certification of home and
school visitors (school social workers) has been accomplished conceptually
and formally, but the impact upon the competency level of home and school
visitors (school social workers) across the state will be minimal as long
as there is a lack of standardized preparation programs throughout the
commonwealth. Nor can the State Department of Education discontinue transcript review of certification until this is a reality.

The University of Pittsburgh school of social work certification program
remains a subspecialty within a children and youth specialty which students
may elect as an area of emphasis in their graduate social work preparation.
Evaluation of the program is done through a review committee appointed by
the Department of Education. There has been a gradual decrease in student
attraction to a school social work preparation program, requiring state
certification, but for which there is an extremely limited job market. The
number of students enrolled in the program each school year is approximately
eight. This situation is aggravated by the fact that reciprocity of certification across all states does not exist.

MAINTENANCE STRATEGIES

Since the social work profession is concerned with planned purposeful intervention to attain problem solution there are, fortunately, constructive
efforts under way to support school social work services of high quality in
our states. For example, at the national level the NASW Practice Advancement
Council on Social Work Services in Schools had made excellent progress in
advancing the professional practice of school social work through encouraging
research in many areas of school social work practice; through lobbying in
the political arena for maintenance of quality school social services; and
through promoting publication which addresses school, family, and child
needs.

Annual regional school social work conferences afford increased knowledge
among practitioners and educators relative to effective and innovative
school social work programs. Such conferences should be considered for
initiation in regions throughout the nation, since they also provide a
vehicle for educating and gaining support of the general public around the
importance of quality school social work services. In many states,
including the state of Pennsylvania, state governors have been persuaded
to declare a school social work week or day as a way of recognizing school
social workers. Helping to educate the community about school social work
services must be an ongoing process for all social workers.

In reference to Pennsylvania specifically, the Pennsylvania Association
of School Social Work Personnel (PASSWP) was organized in 1979, to advance
the provision of quality social work services in the schools. Members of
the PASSWP have spearheaded efforts to gain legislative support for
improved school social work programs. Through collaborative planning with

the Pennsylvania Department of Education, PASSWP has organized state and local conferences to address school social work issues, preparation, and services. The department has responded to this organizational effort by requesting consultation from PASSWP on preparation standards and general interpretation of school social services in view of new legislation such as P.L. 94-142 (Education for All Handicapped Children Act), school desegregation laws, and changing societal trends such as the increasing single-parent families. Demands for new knowledge and improved competencies for meeting changing needs of pupils, families and schools are being identified and interpreted by practitioners and educators at both state and local educational agency levels in an effort to assure quality preparation and services. Nevertheless, without a qualified representative for school social workers on the pupil personnel (student services) committee, the control for decision-making in relation to competencies required for certification generally will remain outside of the social work profession. The Department of Education and the schools of education collaborate in maintaining ultimate decision-making power about the overall organization of the program and the certification process. This is of particular significance when it is noted that the new state Department of Education plan shows increased emphasis upon instructional services and decreased emphasis in human services as reflected in a recent Pennsylvania Department of Education proposal to eliminate the student services division.

Further, the Pennsylvania State chapter of NASW is organized around the issue of promoting licensing of social workers in Pennsylvania. If licensing is approved for social workers who practice in Pennsylvania, it will be necessary to evaluate the relationship between state licensing and state certification processes and preparation programs in respect to title, role, and function of school social workers.

CONCLUSION

Developmental dilemmas experienced by the University of Pittsburgh in providing and maintaining a home and school visitor (school social work) preparation program should be of particular significance to faculty, students, and practitioners engaged in similar efforts. There must be strong commitment at federal, state, and local levels to the critical need for high-quality social work services and expertise in school settings. Failure to gain this commitment, particularly during an economically depressed state of our nation, results in fiscal restraints and increased turf protecting by the profession of education, which seriously affect the allocation of resources for human service preparation programs. Inter-related with problems of insufficient representation of qualified school social workers at state department level, low public commitment, and declining economy are circumstances such as the deterioration of inner cities, shifts in communities, declining enrollment, and changing neighbor-hoods, leaving some school districts seriously impoverished and resulting in stringent job losses for many school personnel. This is particularly true for professional school social workers, whose services are frequently classified as "frills" to the educational system during periods of a budgetary crunch.

NOTES AND REFERENCES

1.   Jack A.N. Ellis and Vernon E. Bryant, "Competency-based Certification for School Social Workers," Social Work, 21 (September 1976), p. 381.

2.   Ibid., pp. 381-382.

3.   Mable T. Emanuel Hawkins, State Standards for Certificated School Social Worker, Visiting Teacher, Attendance Worker, and Home-School Visitor, Publication No. 79-24, 716; school: University of Pittsburgh (Ann Arbor, Mich.: University Microfilms International, 1979).

4.   Ibid., pp. 154-156.

5.   Mable T. Emanuel Hawkins, A Survey of State Certification Standards for School Social Workers, Home School Visitors, Visiting Teachers, and Attendance Workers (Bethesda, Md.: ERIC Document Reproduction Service, ED 185452, 1980). (Note school social work preparation program and certification requirements for the following states: New Jersey, Michigan, Wisconsin, Nebraska, Kentucky, Colorado, California, Washington, Alaska, Illinois, Georgia, and Pennsylvania.

6.   "Summary of Responses to Questionnaires Completed by Graduate Schools of Social Work," Appendix B (Salt Lake City: University of Utah Graduate School of Social Work, 1976). (Mimeographed.)

7.   Ibid.

8.   Mable T. Hawkins, "Developmental Dilemmas of a State Approved, University Sponsored Home and School Visitor Program." Paper presented at the annual program meeting of the Council on Social Work Education, Philadelphia, Pa., 1976. (Mimeographed.)

9.   Policies, Procedures and Standards for Certification of Professional School Personnel (Pennsylvania Department of Education, 1974), pp. 87-88.

10.   Ibid., p. 87.

11.   Elizabeth H. Woellner, Requirements for Certification for Elementary Schools, Secondary Schools, Junior Colleges (39th ed.; Chicago: University of Chicago Press, 1974).

12.   Program Description, Home and School Visitor Certificate, Pennsylvania Department of Education, Commonwealth of Pennsylvania (Pittsburgh: University of Pittsburgh, 1975), p. 22.

13.   Ibid.

14.   Report of a Visiting Committee from the Department of Education for Graduate Programs for the Preparation of Home and School Visitors (Pittsburgh: University of Pittsburgh School Guidance Services, 1972), p. 15.

15. Anne V. Ginevan, "The Evolution of the Home and School Visitor Services in Pittsburgh Public Schools: Sociological and Economic Influences." Unpublished doctoral dissertation, University of Pittsburgh, Pittsburgh, Pa., 1974.

16. Jeffrey Shelton, "Paraprofessional Attendance Workers: Implications for School Social Work," Journal of International Association for Pupil Personnel Workers, 19 (March 1975), p. 73.

EVALUATION OF A PROGRAM TO PREPARE
PRACTITIONERS FOR SOCIAL WORK
IN SCHOOL SETTINGS

ALICE E. LAMONT AND BETTY L. WELSH

In 1971 Michigan passed the Mandatory Special Education Act. Since social work was a service component, updated rules and regulations had to be developed based on knowledge and competencies. The authors participated in this revision. Once the law containing the revisions was passed, Wayne State University's School of Social Work, in Detroit, filed an educational plan specifying the means by which candidates would meet the competencies with the State Department of Education (SDE). The MSW curriculum was reviewed and areas which were not covered such as psychological evaluation and the learning process were planned for; two new courses were developed to meet competency requirements in certain areas.

The new rules and regulations for school social work came into effect in 1977. 1/ By 1979, fifty-seven graduates had been hired by local school districts who complied with the new regulations. The authors decided to survey the MSW graduates who had obtained approval for school social work since the revised curriculum had been in place. Such a survey was seen as an opportunity to obtain systematic feedback of the graduates' perception of their preparation and to compare those who had a learning center experience with those who did not. Interest in measuring the effectiveness of the curriculum is a logical development of the trend in social work to be accountable for services promised or implied. Ellis and Bryant describe some of the factors contributing to an accountability set in the wider society, in social work, in education, and especially as experienced by social workers practicing in an educational setting. 2/ Welsh has described this trend and suggested tools for social workers striving to be accountable. 3/ Staff and administrators of social agencies are frequently using or expected to use one of many models for establishing goals and objectives and measuring progress toward them. 4/ And the social work literature has for some time reflected the profession's concerns about documenting the outcome of social work intervention. 5/

All of these efforts toward measuring or somehow accounting for the effectiveness or noneffectiveness of social work were a source of support for examining the outcome of the programs which prepare students for practice. If practitioners are to be held accountable for their practice efforts then it seems only reasonable that educators attempt to measure the effectiveness of education programs which prepare for social work practice.

Two questions are formulated to guide this study of effectiveness of preparation: (1) are MSW graduates (of Wayne State University School of Social Work) prepared in the competencies specified in the rules and regulations and (2) are there implications for curriculum in their experiences? To seek answers to these questions a survey was selected. Since the practitioners were scattered around the metropolitan Detroit area and the state of Michigan a written survey seemed a practical method of asking for their feedback.

A questionnaire was designed utilizing the knowledge, skills, and competencies statements specified in the state's official rules and regulations. 6/ The eighteen questions varied from asking respondents to rate their preparation for diagnosis-assessment of the individual to asking them to rate their knowledge of current legislation affecting social workers and schools, specifying four different laws or regulations. With the subparts of questions, there were forty-one items on preparation and forty-one on usefulness. Each respondent was asked to rank the adequacy of his or her preparation in this subject, that is, the learning process, from one (low) to five (high). For some knowledge or skill or competency statements subparts are specified. For example, for diagnosis-assessment of social functioning, the respondent was asked to rate his or her preparation for individuals, families, small groups, classrooms, and community.

In addition to the level of preparation of the graduates of the program the researchers were interested in knowing how useful this knowledge had been to them on the job. In order to obtain the respondent's assessment of usefulness, a second part was designed for each question: "How useful has this knowledge and skill been in your practice in the school?" The respondents were instructed to rank the usefulness from one (low) to five (high). The third aspect of great interest to the researchers was the respondents' perception of the source of their preparation. Where had they learned it? Was one part of the curriculum more influential than another? Three possible sources were listed: class, field, and learning center. A space was provided to write in other sources, such as previous experience. 7/ The following is an example of a question and directions.

Please circle the number which best represents your preparation for knowing the structure and organization of schools, and circle the letter which indicates the source of that preparation.

preparation	source	(please specify
1 2 3 4 5	FP SLC C	if class or other)

How useful has this knowledge and skill been as you began practice in the school?

1 2 3 4 5

The sample consisted of all those MSW graduates from the School of Social Work at Wayne State University who had been employed by various school districts as social workers since the revised rules and regulations were put into effect in the fall of 1977. Most of the sample consisted of recent graduates. It did include a few persons who had graduated earlier and recently completed the requirements for approval as school social workers. The characteristics of the respondents are reported in Table 1. The majority of the respondents were under 35 years old, had majored in social casework, and had been employed one or two years in a suburban school district. All but two had participated in the Schools Learning Center.

Surveys were mailed to the graduates at the end of the summer in 1979, the authors thinking that the school social workers would have time at the beginning of the school year to respond. The questionnaires with a self-addressed return envelope were sent to either a home or school address. The cover letter signed by the two authors explained that completing the questionnaire would take about fifteen or twenty minutes. The letter also indicated that a similar questionnaire would be sent to department directors for feedback on the graduates' preparation unless a graduate asked to have the director's name removed from the list. No graduates asked to have the director's name omitted. However, subsequent mechanical difficulties made it impossible to survey the directors.

Fifty-six questionnaires were mailed. Six were returned because of a wrong address or no forwarding address, one graduate wrote to say she was not in school social work. A follow-up postcard was sent to all in the sample. Twenty-one usable questionnaires were returned. The findings from those replies are reported here.

To address the question, "Are MSW graduates adequately prepared to meet the state competencies?" the mean ratings for preparation for all items were calculated. There was a total of forty-two variables or items for preparation and a similar number for usefulness. Table 2 shows the ten items on which respondents reported their preparation as highest. The phrases are taken from the questionnaire. The ten items reported cover a variety of areas. (Two items are tied in seventh place.) Six items seem related to direct service--utilizing social work knowledge and skills with parents and pupils, assessing needs of adults and adolescents, and diagnosing and treating the individual. Two items have to do with knowledge of current legislation and one is on developing resources outside of school and one on integrating value considerations. All of the items rank between 4.28 and 4.48 on a five-point scale. From this table it appears that the graduates feel fairly well prepared for direct practice and knowledgeable about the Michigan's Mandatory Special Education Act, and the federal Education for All Handicapped Children Act (P.L. 94-142).

Table 3 presents the items on which the respondents reported themselves as least prepared. The items are clustered in roughly four groups. The first three items are related to specific impairments--speech, sensory, and physical and the fourth item is on the federal Rehabilitation Act of 1973--all of which appear to be related. The other grouping for this bottom ranking are community (two items), small groups and classroom (three items and one item), and developing service priorities with an administrator.

(Text continues on page 85.)

Table 1. Characteristics of Respondents

Age	Under 35		Between 35-45		46 or Over
	13		4		4

Year of MSW	Prior to 1970	1976	1977	1978	1979
	2	1	7	10	1

MSW major	Casework	Group Work	Social Work Practice
	16	4	2 a/

Other methods studied		
	4	1

Years as school social worker	1-2 yrs.	3-4 yrs.	5-6 yrs.	7 yrs. or more
	14	3	2	2

Participant in learning center on social work in school systems	Yes	No
	19	2

Field experience in a school setting	Yes	No
	17	4

Field experience in a child oriented setting	19	2

Work experience with children	19	2

Setting of employment	Surburban	Urban	Rural
	14	5	2

a/ One respondent reported two methods.

Table 2. The Ten Content Knowledge Items on Which Recently Approved School Social Workers Rated Themselves as Most Prepared

	Rank	Mean Score a/
Utilizing social work knowledge and skill in interaction with parents	1	4.48
Knowing current legislation affecting social workers and schools--P.A. 198 (Mandatory Special Education Act) b/	2	4.47
Assessing clients' needs at various developmental stages--adults	3	4.45
Identifying and developing resources outside of school	4	4.40
Knowing current legislation affecting social workers and schools--P.L. 94-142 (Education for All Handicapped Children Act)	5	4.37
Utilizing social work knowledge and skills in interactions with pupils	6	4.35
Treating-interviewing individual	7	4.32
Diagnosis-assessment of social functioning--individual	7	4.32
Assessing clients' needs at various developmental stages--adolescence	8	4.30
Integrating value considerations into plans for service of the clients, school, society, and self	9	4.28

a/ Rating scale was from 1 (low) to 5 (high).
b/ Michigan.

It is interesting to note the mean scores for this group. The scores range from 2.10 to 3.35 on a five-point scale. The midpoint for such a scale is 2.5. Only one item, related to speech impairment, is rated below the midpoint. From this one might conclude that the respondents considered themselves at least moderately well prepared on every one of the forty-two items listed in the questionnaire with just one exception. So far the

Table 3. The Ten Content Knowledge Items on Which Recently Approved School
Social Workers Rated Themselves as Least Prepared

	Rank a/	Mean Score b/
Development of educational plans with school personnel for people with speech impairments	36	2.10
Development of educational plans with school personnel for pupils with sensory impairments	35	2.68
Development of educational plans with school personnel for pupils with physical impairments	35	2.68
Knowing current legislation--P.L. 93-112 (Rehabilitation Act of 1973)	34	2.73
Diagnosis-assessment of social functioning of community	33	2.94
Treating-intervening in small groups	32	3.15
Diagnosis-assessment of social functioning of classroom	31	3.16
Treating-intervening in community	30	3.21
Assessing socioemotional needs of a school	29	3.23
Diagnosis-assessment of social functioning of small groups	28	3.28
Mutually developing with an administrator, priorities for service based upon a needs assessment	27	3.35

a/ With ties there are 36 ranks for the 40 items.
b/ Rating scale from 1 (low) to 5 (high).

tables have reported the respondents' perception of their preparation. The
next two tables comment on the usefulness of the items to the respondents
as they began to practice in schools. In Table 4, the ten items ranked as
most useful are reported.

The ten most useful items appear to be clustered into two groups: direct and indirect practice. One item is in a third category: legislation

Table 4. The Ten Content-Knowledge Items Which Recently Approved School
Social Workers Rated as Most Useful

	Rank	Mean Score a/
Utilizing social work knowledge and skills in interactions with parents	1	4.8
Utilizing social work knowledge and skills in interactions with teachers	2	4.7
Understanding the use of psychological evaluation in collaborative planning and communication with members of other disciplines and parents	3	4.66
Knowing the structure and organization of schools	3	4.66
Utilizing social work knowledge and skills in interactions with pupils	4	4.65
Utilizing social work knowledge and skills in interactions with administration	5	4.61
Assessing client needs at various developmental stages--adults	5	4.61
Diagnosis-assessment social functioning--individual	6	4.60
Utilizing social work knowledge and skills in interactions with team members	7	4.57
Knowing current legislation affecting social workers and schools--P.A. 198 (Mandatory Special Education Act) b/	7	4.57

a/ Rating scale was from 1 (low) to 5 (high).
b/ Michigan.

(the Mandatory Special Education Act). The four related to direct practice
are: utilizing social work knowledge and skills with parents and pupils;
assessing client needs at various developmental stages--adults; and diagnosis-assessment of social functioning--individual. The five items which
seem related to indirect practice needs are utilizing social work knowledge
and skills with teachers, administration, and team members; understanding
the use of psychological evaluation in collaborative planning and communication with members of other disciplines and parents; and knowing the

Table 5. The Ten Content-Knowledge Items Which the Recently Approved
School Social Workers Rated as Least Useful

	Rank	Mean Score
Knowing current legislation affecting social workers and schools--P.L. 93-112 (Rehabilitation Act of 1973)	30 a/	2.80 b/
Developing educational plans with school personnel for pupils with speech impairments	29	2.95
Utilizing research and evaluation in your practice	28	3.33
Developing educational plans with school personnel for pupils with sensory impairments	27	3.57
Developing educational plans with school personnel for pupils with physical impairments	27	3.57
Assessing client needs at various developmental stages--infancy	26	3.60
Treating-intervening--small groups	25	3.61
Treating-intervening--community	24	3.71
Diagnosis-assessment of social functioning--classrooms	23	3.80
Assessing socioemotional needs of a school	23	3.80

a/ With ties there are 30 ranks for the 40 items.
b/ Rating scale from 1 (low) to 5 (high).

structure and organization of schools. It appears that content regarding indirect work in schools is rated somewhat more useful than the direct service items which made up more than half of the items on the most prepared list. However, this distinction is quite speculative, since items categorized as direct service such as diagnosis-assessment--individuals might be equally useful to the practitioners in indirect service, that is, with team members or administrators. In terms of scores, all of the ten "useful" items in Table 4 are rated higher than the "preparation" items in Table 2.

The next aspect considered are those items which landed at the bottom of the usefulness rating. The ten items, reported in Table 5, seemed dispersed over five categories. The least useful items are related to three impairments--speech, sensory, and physical; two are related to small groups and the classroom; and one each to the school, community, infancy, research, and the Rehabilitation Act. In terms of mean scores, all are rated above the midpoint of 2.5 and range as high as 3.80, suggesting there are no content items which the new practitioners did not find useful.

The second major question posed in the study was, "What are the implications for curriculum?" The respondents' ratings of preparation items provide information in part for that question. Another dimension of preparation of interest to the researchers was the source. Where do students learn about certain things? Is it class or field or the combination that makes for the best prepared most useful information? To pursue this, the items which rated highest in both preparation and usefulness were grouped and the source of learning for each analyzed. The same procedure was carried out for those lowest in both preparation and usefulness. The two were then compared for any differences in preparation.

In Table 6, the six items that were in the top group for both preparation and usefulness are reported along with the source for each item. Four of the items appear to relate to direct service, one to legislation, one to indirect service. Sources of learning appear quite diverse although class and field are reported as sources of learning almost three times as often as are the learning center or other sources.

The curriculum plan to meet the competencies which is filed with the SDE lists several sources by which to meet most of the competencies. The findings are consistent with this plan. In Table 7 the items rated lowest in both preparation and usefulness are arrayed along with the sources of learning reported for each item. Among the eight items, there is again the cluster of the three impairments and the Rehabilitation Act, and small groups, the classroom, school, and community. In a visual inspection of sources of learning the items rated high in Table 6 seemed to have a richer mix of sources. In examining the totals for each column and row, however, a much different pattern appears. The grand totals are very close for both the high and low groups, 160 and 167. There are even a few more sources reported for the low items. There is very little difference in the total number of times class and learning center are reported as sources. There is, however, a considerable difference in field and other.

Fieldwork is cited as a source of learning 69 times on the highly rated items compared to 50 times on the low-rated items. "Other" is cited as a source of learning only 21 times on the high items and 40 times on the low items. The similarity in frequency of class and learning center sources for both high and low items suggests that encountering these items in the field may be the chief difference in how it is ranked. Although the questionnaires were not analyzed for other responses for this report one suspects that on the job and life experiences are important factors.

(Text continues on page 92.)

Table 6. Sources of Content-Knowledge Items Rated High on Both Preparation and Usefulness

Rank in Usefulness	Rank in Preparation	Content-Knowledge	Source				
			Class	Field	L.C.a/	Other	Total b/
1	1	Utilizing social work knowledge and skills--parents	7	15	4	2	28
4	6	Utilizing social work knowledge and skills--pupils	6	14	4	3	27
5	10	Utilizing social work knowledge and skill--administration	6	12	3	6	27
5	3	Assessing client needs--developmental stages--adults	10	13	0	3	26
6	7	Diagnosis-assessment of functioning--individual	14	11	0	2	27
7	2	Knowing current legislation--P.A. 198 (Mandatory Special Education Act)	11	4	6	5	26
		TOTAL	54	69	17	21	161

a/ Learning center.
b/ More than one choice was possible as the source for learning, so totals may be greater than the number of respondents (21).

90

Table 7. Sources of Content-Knowledge Items Rated Low on Both Preparation and Usefulness

Rank in Usefulness	Rank in Preparation	Content-Knowledge	Source				Total
			Class	Field	L.C. a/	Other	
30 b/	34 c/	Knowing current legislation--P.L. 93-112 (Rehabilitation Act of 1973)	6	3	3	3 d/	15
29	36	Developing educational plans with school personnel for pupils with speech impairments	4	7	0	7 f/	18
27	35	Developing educational plans with school personnel for pupils with sensory impairments	7	6	1	7 e/	21
27	35	Developing educational plans with school personnel for pupils with physical impairments	7	7	0	8 e/	22
25	32	Treating-intervening--small groups	7	9	1	2	19
24	30	Treating-intervening--community	7	7	5	5	24
23	31	Diagnosis-assessment of functioning--classroom	8	4	5	5	22
23	29	Assessing socioemotional needs of a school	11	7	5	3	26
		TOTAL	57	50	20	40	167

a/ Learning center. b/ Lowest rank for usefulness is 30. c/ Lowest rank for preparation is 36. d/ Six no answer, perhaps related to level of information. e/ One response missing. f/ Four responses missing.

91

DISCUSSION

This follow-up study of graduates from one school of social work who qualified for employment in a school system within a three-year period describes their perceptions of their preparation on the items drawn from the state rules and regulations. There are several aspects which limit the generalizability of the study. The sample consisted of twenty-one respondents, less than half of those receiving questionnaires. All but two of the respondents had been part of the learning center, making it impractical to study any differences in the preparation of learning center and non-learning center students. Since the students in the learning center work closely with faculty their relationships with the authors may have been a factor in their responding. The other respondents may not have had sufficient motivation to answer the eighteen-question, ten-page questionnaire.

In considering the two main questions of the study: (1) Do the newly approved graduates perceive themselves as prepared in the competencies? and (2) Are there implications for curriculum?--the answers seem to be yes. The respondents rated their preparation above the midpoint on all but one item, a surprisingly high rating considering the diversity of items contained in the rules and regulations. It is important to note that there is no scale for determining level of competency in the state's rules and regulations; this study is based on self-reports. Although prepared on almost all items the graduates tended to report the highest preparation on direct service items, not surprising since the great majority were casework and group work majors, and on two pieces of legislation. In terms of usefulness their responses were more evenly divided between direct and indirect service and all items were rated above the midpoint on usefulness, suggesting they were able to use everything they learned.

The implications for curriculum seem to be (1) a greater emphasis on sensory, speech, and physical impairments and the Rehabilitation Act, on small groups, school as a system and community and (2) attention to these items in the practicum. Replication of the study, or a modified version, with succeeding classes and further efforts to reach most graduates seems warranted in view of the findings. Even with its limitations this study does provide useful feedback on the preparation of students for practice in schools.

NOTES AND REFERENCES

1. Rules and Regulations for School Social Work (R 340.1011 to R 340.1018), Michigan State Department of Education, approved by the State Board of Education, August 1977.

2. Jack A.N. Ellis and Vernon E. Bryant, "Competency-Based Certification for School Social Workers," Social Work, 21 (September 1976), pp. 381-385.

3. Betty L. Welsh, "An Interdisciplinary Systems Approach to Accountability," <u>Social Work in Education</u>, 1 (July 1979), pp. 44-54.

4. Melvyn C. Raider, "A Social Service Model of Management by Objectives," <u>Social Casework</u>, 57 (October 1976), pp. 523-528.

5. Katherine M. Wood, "Casework Effectiveness: A New Look at the Research Evidence," <u>Social Work</u>, 23 (November 1978), pp. 437-458.

6. <u>Rules and Regulations for School Social Work</u>, op. cit.

7. Michael Roche contributed to the literature review for the study and material for the instrument.

DEPLOYMENT AND EDUCATION
OF SCHOOL SOCIAL WORKERS

Lynn Corbin, C. Richard Donahue,
and Wallace Lornell

Graduate schools of social work, like many other graduate schools, have
been criticized by practitioners for not adequately preparing workers for
the kinds of problems they face when they begin a practice. While recognizing
the importance of generic training for social workers and the danger of
fragmenting the social work profession, it is essential that schools of
social work reappraise the public schools as a special field of practice.
Few graduate schools of social work present a focused curriculum for the
preparation of social workers to practice in public school settings. The
report of the joint Council on Social Work Education/National Association
of Social Workers task force on specialization in practice described some of
the issues related to the education of school social workers.

School social work practitioners themselves have different opinions
about the education of school social workers. Many school social workers
contend that the MSW degree is insufficient to practice in the public schools
because the public school is an interdisciplinary setting which requires
special knowledge and skills. They also content that school social workers
need to know about learning theory, schools as an institution, psychological
and educational testing, educational law, and those laws pertaining to
compulsory education of handicapped children. Most school social workers
do not have access to supervision or consultation, and it is difficult for
them to acquire this information while on the job. Many school social workers
are of the opinion that a fieldwork placement in the public school should be
required.

Other school social workers contend that the MSW degree with the generic
training is sufficient preparation for the practice of school social work.
They feel that it is specifically the knowledge of community resources,
social agencies, and of interviewing skills which public schools find so
valuable in the preparation of the social worker. They further state that
school administrators look to the school social worker to make a contribution
in these listed areas rather than in the technical areas of education, as such.
The contention is made that the social worker can learn about the setting on
the job and that the employer is responsible to provide orientation and
consultation for new employees.

BACKGROUND

In New York State, school social work is practiced in two general areas.
It is practiced in urban areas, including major cities such as New York
and smaller cities, such as White Plains. It is also practiced in surburban
rural areas that are found adjacent to the major and minor cities. School
social workers who practice in cities are frequently members of school
social work departments which function within larger pupil personnel
structures. These departments usually include school social work supervisors,
and there is a provision for a hierarchy of social work accountability,
evaluation, and professional development. In some cities, the model for
social work within the school is that of a mental health specialist who
provides the school with mental health services. More often, the model
within cities is that of a social worker who functions as part of the total
school structure and is, in fact, a school social worker.

The school social worker who practices in the suburban-rural area
functions independently as part of a small pupil personnel team and, in
fact, is identified as a school social worker. The social worker who
functions in this area has no formal supervision or opportunity for evaluation or professional development by a supervising social worker or clinician.
Usually, the social worker in the suburban-rural school is accountable to
an administrator who is a former teacher.

While the social worker functioning in the most city schools responds
to problems that are communicated in a more formal way through pupil personnel
services, the social worker functioning in the suburban-rural area responds
directly to the needs of the entire school community. These needs most often
include the daily social, emotional and educational needs of children.
However, they frequently represent the needs of parents, teacher, schools,
and the community at large. The school worker in this suburban-rural
school works alone to define and partialize the problems presented, and
there is little opportunity for dialogue with professional colleagues.

The social work intern placed in a city school is frequently one of
several interns participating in a fieldwork placement. However, the
social work intern placed in the suburban-rural school usually functions
in isolation from other students. The intern functions with considerable
independence and experiences the same isolation that is experienced by the
certified social worker. The nature of this placement requires an intern
of unusual maturity and ability.

SUPERVISING A SOCIAL WORK INTERN IN A SUBURBAN-RURAL SCHOOL

An example of the experience of a social work supervisor and a social work
intern placed in a suburban-rural school district involves preparation which
often exceeds that of the placement of an intern in a social work setting.
The case of a placement of this nature in a northeastern New York public
school setting is cited.

A contract was signed by the local university and the public school administration indicating the commitment of both to social work training as well as specific policies and procedures between the fieldwork supervisor and the student trainee. This contract included dates of placement, required learning experiences, supervisory time, and the student's role in the program. Scheduled communications between the graduate school of social work and the fieldwork supervisor were stated.

The public school's commitment to training the social work intern, as well as the contractual agreement, were essential in order to facilitate the successful experience of supervising the graduate school social work intern in the educational setting. The complexity, bureaucracy, and size of the public school precluded the need for structure and policies which would maximize the effective delivery of services. Where demands on the time of the school social worker supervisor were great, due to the numbers to be serviced and the program's multiple needs, the administration's commitment to release time for adequate supervision was essential. In addition, the public school administration needed to understand that the student social worker was placed in the public school for learning purposes, not to fill caseload demands. The interpretation of the student's role was clarified so that it would be understood by the school board and the administration. It was also clarified for other members of the school staff who might assume more services from this intern than would be appropriate. The university staff was informed about the particular school of social work program that existed in this district so that they would be aware of the experiences confronting the social work intern while in training.

Preparation by the supervisor for the student's encounters and learning experiences within the school setting was a slow and gradual process. The supervisor and the student spent more time in the process of orientation than would be easily found in the traditional social work setting. Graduate schools of social work emphasize an understanding of the total child in their training. Social workers are traditionally trained in the areas of human growth and development, ego and behavioral psychology, and, in some cases, systems theory. Graduate schools of social work should provide a curriculum to social work interns in the areas of organizational theory which would include the public school system. Public schools include many areas of specialization within their structure about which practicing school social workers must become familiar in order to work effectively in this setting. Graduate schools do not cover this material, and considerable time is spent by the fieldwork supervisor in helping the intern to understand learning theory, psychological testing, educational evaluations, committees on the handicapped, and educational law. Although this material cannot necessarily be provided in the graduate school of social work, an understanding of the need for this knowledge and of the time spent by the fieldwork supervisor in sharing this knowledge should be understood by the faculty of the graduate school.

A major portion of the fieldwork supervisor's job in training the social work intern is helping the intern to understand the interdisciplinary function of the school social worker. The supervision of an intern must assist that intern in using the group process to clarify his or her role in this capacity. Status questions frequently arise among various persons within the school structure who have responsibility for children in the school program. In the school setting, where the social worker's identity is secure, there is little conflict or confusion. The school social worker must know the skills and values of his or her own profession and then understand the skills and values of those professionals he or she finds working in the public school. Frequently the social work intern discovers that the teacher's value system is contrary to the value system of the social worker. The school social worker understands the differentiation of the roles among the various persons who impact on the child's situation. Considerable time must be spent in role definition and clarification to help the social work intern to establish an identity in order to proceed with the problem-solving process.

Much of the art of school social work practice takes place during the transfer of skills through the experience of coordination, consultation, and collaboration with administrators, teachers and staff. The skill of coordination of client services is one of the most important social work activities. The coordination of the total intervention plan becomes a popular function of the school social worker because that person is knowledge-able concerning the different agencies, programs, and professionals with different areas of expertise and orientations which impact on the client's situation. As much as social workers use this mode of operation, it is conceptualized differently in different settings and it means different things to different people. The skill of coordination as experienced by the school social worker takes place predominantly in the context of the interdisciplinary function. It often expands beyond the boundaries of the school and involves inter- and intraorganizational factors. The training and education in the art of coordination should be expanded upon by the graduate school of social work and receive more emphasis than it is currently given.

In public schools, school social workers consult with the staff on an ongoing and short-term basis on a variety of levels. For example, the skill of consulting with the school administrator to develop an alternative program to suspension of students will call for specific skills on a programmed-centered level, as opposed to the ongoing consultation involved in working with a teacher related to a child's learning problems. Because the teacher is the primary person relating to the child, school social workers need to be able to transfer some of their skills to that teacher in order to change the child's condition. Because of the social worker's diagnostic and assessment skill, appropriate information can be translated to the teacher in order to assist the teacher make changes on behalf of the child.

Finally, it is evident that a significant amount of time is spent in helping the social work intern understand the complexity of the referral process and achieving maximum service on behalf of the child. This complicated process of referral, both within the school and within the community, is another practice issue which is rarely covered adequately in the school of social work.

SOCIAL WORK INTERN

The success of a social work intern depends on at least seven factors. These factors are:

1. The resources the intern brings to the graduate experience.

2. The quality of the education the intern receives at the graduate school.

3. The quality of the experience provided in the fieldwork placement.

4. The relationship that exists between the intern and the graduate school.

5. The relationship that exists between the intern and the fieldwork supervisor.

6. The relationship that exists between the social work intern and the agency (the public school).

7. The relationship between the graduate school faculty and the fieldwork supervisor.

The ideal experience for an intern would be one in which all of these factors operate together to maximize the intern's learning. The factors will operate together when the graduate school faculty and the fieldwork supervisor have a relationship of mutual interest and concern for the intern. This relationship would include an ongoing awareness of the intern's needs and developing potential. This relationship is dependent upon frequent formal and informal communication between the graduate school and the fieldwork supervisor.

The social work intern approaches the first year of graduate school with both awe and apprehension. The intern's awe reflects the perception of the formidable nature of the graduate experience. The intern's apprehension reflects the perception of his or her personal ability to deal with this experience. These feelings of awe and apprehension are shared by all interns, particularly during those early days of graduate school and fieldwork placement. They grow and diminish as the intern begins to deal with faculty members and the fieldwork supervisor. These feelings of awe and apprehension might be viewed as feelings of inadequacy, which will eventually develop into feelings of confidence. All social worker interns entering placement in the public school setting also have feelings based on their own early educational experiences. These feelings may create a special anxiety unique to the public school setting. The exploration of these feelings is a critical part of supervision in this setting.

Anxiety is also a common feeling among all social work interns, and with professional growth this common anxiety develops into creative anxiety. This growth occurs as the intern begins to develop supportive relationships with both the faculty and the fieldwork supervisor. Through contacts with the faculty, the intern is exposed to the why, and through contacts with the fieldwork supervisor, the intern is exposed to the how of social work. The average social work intern will continue to experience both general and specific anxiety in school placement and fieldwork. This anxiety will diminish as achievement and mastery occur.

In the process of helping a social work intern to grow and develop, the responsibilities of the graduate school faculty and the social work supervisor become increasingly critical and involve the need for more frequent communication. The very nature of the process of learning in social work requires that some degree of anxiety exist to help the intern incorporate new skills and develop new insights. It is often important to create anxiety as the process of growth continues. Both the faculty and the supervisor must challenge the social work intern's ability. When the intern's ability is challenged, anxiety is increased, but new competence should develop. As the social work intern experiences new anxiety and achievement, the critical nature of the relationship between the faculty and the supervisor becomes more important. If the social work intern is to grow and develop--if the social work intern is to be stimulated and supported--the graduate school faculty and the fieldwork supervisor must work cooperatively and with an understanding of their respective roles. The faculty and the supervisor cannot work in isolation.

RESPONSIBILITIES OF FIELDWORK AGENCIES

The expectations of schools of social work regarding fieldwork agencies and fieldwork supervisors are defined in writing by each university. A review of the established criteria of several major universities in the New York area reveals that each university has very clear expectations. These expectations are divided into guidelines for agencies and for field-work supervisors. Most universities expect agencies to fulfill the following criteria:

1. The agency should have a broad philosophy of training, which would include the training of social workers; and this philosophy should be shared by both the school of social work and the agency. The agency should have a demonstrated interest in social work education and a general agreement on content.

2. The agency should have an acceptable level of practice.

3. The agency should have a sound administrative structure and should consider within its administrative structure the training of interns. This administrative structure should consider such specific considerations as the availability of office space, telephones, and secretarial staff for social work interns.

4.   The agency should provide for adequate intern supervision and planning. The agency should select supervisors of quality and should make special considerations for these supervisors, related to their new responsibility.

5.   The agency should see that provision is made for an appropriate range and depth of educational contact for the intern. This would consider, for example, that the assignments within the agencies would conform to the school curriculum and that there would be an integration in participation of students into agency activities.

6.   There should be a relationship between the agency and the school that is mutually supportive of the student program.

A review of these criteria established by graduate schools for social work agencies should be made in relation to the unique characteristics of a secondary setting, such as the school, and in particular with consideration of the school setting in a suburban-rural area. Most public schools have had experience in participating with teacher training institutions. Therefore, we might anticipate that they would have some philosophy about training, but this philosophy would not normally include consideration of social work education specifically. In most public schools, particularly in a rural area, social work is practiced by a certified social worker who works in isolation. The level of practice of this social worker is not a factor that is usually assessed by the school in terms of the uniqueness of the school social work function. State certification standards require only that the worker have an MSW.

The administrative structures of most public schools in suburban-rural areas do not provide for the special needs of social work; and in many cases social workers who are functioning in suburban-rural areas do not have easy access to the facilities (such as offices, phones, or secretaries) available to social workers functioning in primary social agencies. The adequacy of student supervisory planning in a suburban-rural public school is usually related to the one social worker who is available in that school, and there is seldom any special consideration given to that social worker for assuming responsibility of supervising a social work intern. The range in depth of educational content in a suburban-rural public school setting is related to the broad experience of the school social worker. This experience is as different as the number of school districts within the state. Any effort to incorporate social work curriculum content and integrate social work practice for the intern is primarily related to the individual efforts of the social worker who is supervising the student. Finally, the relationship that exists between the public school and the graduate school is frequently the relationship that exists between that one school social worker and the faculty member who assumes responsibility as a student field adviser. There is often no relationship between the school as an agency and the graduate school as an institution.

The degree of administrative formality in placement of social work interns in suburban-rural school districts might not go beyond the submission of the intern's name by the fieldwork supervisor to the school board. This procedure fulfills the board's legal requirements regarding certification and liability (that is, a certified school employee must be responsible for the intern). The school board assumes that the school of social work is a responsible institution since it is licensed by the Board of Regents. However, the school board does not require the school of social work to define its responsibilities.

RESPONSIBILITIES OF FIELDWORK SUPERVISORS

The schools of social work are equally specific about their expectations of fieldwork supervisors. These expectations frequently include the following:

1. The social work fieldwork supervisor should be motivated for student supervision and teaching.

2. The fieldwork supervisor should have proven knowledge and skill in practice. Most graduate schools require that a fieldwork supervisor have a master's degree in social work plus two or three years of experience.

3. The fieldwork supervisor should have a mature and stable personality.

4. The fieldwork supervisor should accept the responsibility of an educator.

5. The fieldwork supervisor should have the capacity and ability to teach.

6. The fieldwork supervisor should have the capacity and ability to organize work and plan for educating and supervising the intern.

7. The fieldwork supervisor should have an identification with the objectives of the agency.

8. The fieldwork supervisor should have the capacity and ability to relate to the graduate school and a willingness and ability to attend meetings at the graduate school.

The social worker practicing in a suburban-rural area who functions alone without support or supervision would have to be highly motivated to accept the responsibility of supervising and teaching an intern. The knowledge and skill of the social worker would usually be based on graduate training and experience, but would be unique to this setting, the area and the school in which this worker was practicing. The ability to survive over a period of years working alone in a setting such as we have described often involves a degree of maturity and stability that may not, in fact, be required in a more protective primary setting. The social worker in this setting looks upon the experience of fieldwork not only as an opportunity to train new social workers, but to maintain and improve social work skills already developed by the supervisor.

The capacity to teach is one which may exist, but must be nurtured, not only by the support of the agency, but by the efforts of the school of social work. This is also true of the capacity to organize and plan for the social work intern. The social work supervisor in this type of setting has a split identification, with both the objectives of the agency and the objectives of social work. The ability to bring these identifications together on behalf of a client requires experience and maturity. Finally, the supervisor's capacity and ability to relate to the graduate school is expressed in the supervisor's willingness to accept the graduate intern and initiate the contact with the school. It is dependent, however, on the graduate school's willingness to reciprocate in a sharing relationship.

RESPONSIBILITIES OF SCHOOLS OF SOCIAL WORK

A review of the criteria established by schools of social work indicates that they have, in fact, defined certain responsibilities for themselves. These responsibilities include the following:

1. Preparing summaries to guide the fieldwork instructor.

2. Consulting with the fieldwork instructor to determine needs and prepare evaluations.

3. Providing guidelines for both content of fieldwork and the evaluation of students.

4. The initiation of student review where problems arise.

5. The provision of seminars for fieldwork supervisors.

6. The evaluation of both the agency and fieldwork supervisor on a regular basis.

7. The provision of course outlines to fieldwork supervisors.

8. Provision to the agency and supervisor with information about policies and programs.

The experience of many fieldwork supervisors in school settings reveals that the material provided by the school of social work regarding the social work intern is inadequate and not timely. It would be helpful if detailed material were submitted by the school of social work to the agency supervisor in advance of placement. This material would include a social history on the intern, a copy of university policy regarding fieldwork, and a curriculum outline. This material would outline the responsibilities of the faculty adviser assigned to the student intern, the name of the adviser, and the dates of the adviser's scheduled visits. The curriculum outline would be detailed to include the types of material the student would learn and the approximate time when this material would be given to the student.

The unique nature of the fieldwork placement in the suburban-rural school requires planned involvement between the school faculty adviser and the fieldwork supervisor. This involvement would include the following:

1. An early visit prior to placement of the proposed social work intern, for consideration by the agency supervisor.

2. An early visit by the faculty adviser following an "early written assessment" by the supervisor. This early assessment would expedite the intern's growth and development.

3. A written response by the school of social work to the early assessment, indicating the student's progress in school.

4. A midyear visit by the faculty adviser in conjunction with the midyear evaluation.

5. Written response to the midyear evaluation to indicate the faculty assessment for this student.

6. A final visit by the faculty adviser prior to the final evaluation.

7. A written assessment for the student's academic progress to be submitted to the fieldwork supervisor.

A discussion among school social workers who have either supervised social work interns in a school setting or have, in fact, been social work interns in a school setting resulted in additional proposed criteria for graduate schools in fulfilling the responsibilities in relation to the school as an agency and the school social worker as a fieldwork supervisor. Some of the criteria that were suggested include the following:

1. Participation by a faculty member from the school of social work in agency activities. This might include a visit by the faculty members to a meeting of the Committee on the Handicapped, to board meetings, faculty meetings, or meetings of the pupil personnel staff.

2. Faculty status and recognition for the experienced school social worker who functions as a fieldwork supervisor.

3. Representation of experienced school social work/fieldwork supervisors on university committees.

4.   Involvement of experienced supervisors in course presentations that are related to school social work. These activities would involve some nominal honorarium.

5.   Eligibility of experienced supervisors for post-master's-degree courses at the school of social work without cost.

6.   Provision of special training programs for supervisors at the school of social work at no cost. These would be organized at a convenient time and would offer post-master's-degree credit.

7.   Special recognition of the public school as an agency used by the school of social work. This might involve a personal letter from the dean of the school of social work to the superintendent of schools.

8.   Recognition of the special needs of interns who are placed in school settings. This might involve such things as special seminars for students in school settings. Schools of social work might cooperate together in forming discussion groups among their students who are having the same experience in school so that they could share both the joy and disappointment that is part of school social work.

SUMMARY AND CONCLUSIONS

The New York State Education Department and the New York State School Social Workers Association are concerned about the problems that exist in the training of social workers and are making every effort to communicate with schools of social work that have accredited social work programs. Their mutual concerns have included the following:

1.   The continued definition of school social in a narrow clinical model by some of the school of social work.

2.   The general concept of differentiated staffing and the role of the BSW social worker in the delivery of school social work services.

3.   The apparent lack of understanding on the part of schools of social work regarding the definition of the role and tasks of the school social worker.

4.   The inadequacy of information on the practice of school social

5.   The problem created by the wide variety of roles of school social work and the problems this creates for schools of social work.

6.   The fact that child welfare workers and mental health workers have frequent contact with schools, but get little information in the graduate curriculum interpreting the public school as an institution in our society.

7. The fact that no graduate schools of social work in New York State encourage or permit graduate students to take pertinent courses in schools of education located on the same campuses.

8. The assignment of fieldwork supervisors who have no knowledge of school social work.

9. The lack of commitment by some school social work practitioners to the supervision and training of social work interns.

10. The need for graduate schools to become familiar with federal legislation for handicapped children which requires schools to provided services previously provided by other agencies.

11. The need for graduate schools of social work to be aware of the implications for the future employment of school social workers made by new state and federal legislation.

12. Need for school social workers to update and improve their skills and knowledge, and provide access to continuing education in a practical manner.

In New York State, social workers have been employed in public schools for over eighty years. During the past two decades, the importance of this involvement has increased. The public school has recognized its responsibility to provide special services to many new groups of students. These special services frequently include the use of school social work. The future will see an increased need for competent, mature, and experience social workers who are willing to work in the public schools. Many social workers who are employed in public schools work alone and in isolation. They are the only representatives within this setting who possess the unique and important skills that are part of this social work function.

Schools of social work do not adequately prepare social workers to function in this type of setting. The very nature of the training experience makes it almost impossible for the schools of social work to incorporate all of the material and all of the experiences that would be necessary for a social worker to learn to function with the degree of independence and competence required in a school setting. However, opportunities exist within school districts adjacent to schools of social work where interns can begin to identify and develop the unique skills required of this work. These opportunities can only be exploited through a new effort on the part of individual social workers functioning in the public school and the faculties of schools of social work to reach out to each other. This process will take sacrifice and accommodation, but it will provide interns with professional experience and children with professional service.

THE NONBIASED SOCIAL ASSESSMENT

Elizabeth L. McKinney and Ray H. MacNair

The social assessment has long been an integral part of social work practice, and written material about the social assessment has long appeared in social work literature. The practical issue of a nonbiased social assessment has never been fully resolved.

This article offers a conceptual discussion of the nonbiased social assessment--including definitions of the key terms, ecological theory as an appropriate knowledge base for a nonbiased social assessment, and three questions that may be asked to determine bias in the assessment. Then, the article presents an instrument designed particularly for assessing the social functioning of children and adolescents. It is a bias-reducing instrument. Included here are the process by which the instrument was formulated, its organization and key features, and its use in school social work practice.

DEFINITION OF SOCIAL ASSESSMENT

Social assessment is the process of observation and classification by which social workers determine how the social environment and the client fit and function with one another. The social assessment may be thought of as a study, a diagnosis, evaluation, and analysis. However, Hollis cautions against confusing these terms. She says that the "study" is opening the eyes to see and the "diagnosis" is closing the eyes to think. 1/ Here, the reference is to a process which begins with the first time the social worker becomes aware of the problem, through the analysis of the problem situation, through the development of a plan of intervention to alleviate the problem, and ending with criteria for evaluating the helping process. One can differentiate "social assessment" from "social history" by thinking of social history as a chronology of events that preceded the identified problem. This assessment process seeks to understand social functioning as it is occurring in the here-and-now moment. In assessing the fit and function of client and environment, it is necessary to isolate "social" from other facets of the child; such as, mental, psychological, spiritual, and physical. Social assessment is only one facet of the total assessment. School social workers might think of social assessment as the process by which it is determined if something in the child's social life is hindering learning; if so, what it is and what should be done about it.

Perhaps the uniqueness of the social work assessment can be summarized in two notions. First, a social picture is drawn in cooperation with the client. This notion stems from the value that each client, as a unique individual, is capable of self-determination. Social workers strive toward practice in ways that promote the client's growth in self-determination. Professionals cannot know many of the client's experiences and feelings in a social situation as the client knows them. Therefore, assessment is dependent upon information from the client's verbal and behavioral communications. Social work assessment begins to help the client communicate the necessary information and put the information into forms that can be used in the helping process.

The second notion that makes this kind of assessment unique is that the assessment is conducted simultaneously with the process of giving help. Professional social work intervention is guided by knowledge; it is planned intervention; it is orderly, systematic, and purposeful. Yet, the intervention must start before there can be an intervention plan.

For example, from the beginning, the worker can communicate acceptance of the client as a human being who is in a hurting social situation. The worker can support those behaviors that strengthen the client. The worker can show care and concern for the client. The worker can convey the vision of an eventual solution to the problem. These practices might, in fact, begin raising the social functioning of the client. In essence, the work that goes on simultaneously with developing the assessment is the same work that is part of beginning to establish a helping relationship.

Thus, the school social worker's assessment contributes a specialized kind of knowledge to the plan for the child's growth in learning. In the uniqueness of the social work assessment lies the foundation for the roles and functions of school social workers. With ideas about the school social worker's assessment established, the need now is in establishing the meaning of the term "nonbiased."

THE CONCEPT OF BIAS

The position of this article is that pure "nonbias" is impossible; therefore, the more accurate expression is "less-biased." Movement toward nonbias is accomplished as the value biases are recognized and stated as such. Furthermore, this article notes a conceptual difference between "nonbiased" and "value-free." Workers believe and practice in accordance with a definite set of values. Hence, this article reinforces social assessment from professionally accepted and supported social work values. As will be seen in the later discussion of the assessment instrument, higher levels of social functioning involve behaviors that demonstrate individual autonomy in decision-making and life-style planning, acceptance of human differences, intimacy in family relationships, motivation for success in school, positive self-identity, physical and mental health, and other such values.

The term "bias," on the other hand, suggests a slant, a proclivity, or an inclination toward one side of a question or issue. Social work values, in fact, oppose bias. For example, the profession of social work holds

close emotional relationships in families as a value, but would not bias
the structure, function, habits, and customs of a given family. The task
of the nonbiased social assessment is to reinforce preferred values without
communicating a prejudice regarding issues, questions, and decisions that be-
long to the client. Because of the need for this distinction, these authors
view social assessment through the concepts of ecological theory.

ECOLOGICAL THEORY

According to Cowles, "ecosystem" is a generic term that originated in the
biological sciences and has been used in a broad descriptive sense for almost a century. 2/ Psychologists have used ecological concepts in a wide
variety of studies relating to human populations in social environments;
such as, social institutions, communities, and mental health programs. The
basic premise of ecological theories is their whole systems approach to human interaction. The person is seen as a multifaceted individual in dynamic
interaction with a social environment.

As Wohlwill observed, human behavior is best understood in its context.
Regardless of whether or not motivation is internal and environment is
viewed as the arena for acting and regardless of the issue of whether the
individual or the environment exerts more influence, the premise is that individual and environment interact with one another. 3/ Social assessment
seeks to understand and explain this interaction.

Ecosystems are composed of interdependent populations and their related
environments. These constitute a definable unitary system. For example, in
an assessment of a child's family life, the defined system consists of the
family members within the home environment. If the assessment includes the
neighborhood, the defined system extends to include neighbors and other social units within the environment of the neighborhood. Further assessment
may include the school. The system then extends to include person and place
units within the school environment.

This definition presents certain difficulties, for all population variables and all environmental variables are interactive and could, theoreti-
cally, be included for study. Further, ecosystems vary greatly in size and
complexity. Therefore, the assessment tool presented here defines the boundaries to be studied and selects specific variables. The relationships observed are interpreted as a set of relationships within a context of other
significant interactions. With this approach, it is possible to specify variables which are directly related to the needs of a given assessment. Parts
of an assessment which may be pertinent to one client can be omitted for another without harm to the assessment. Parts are not necessarily assessed in
the order in which they are presented.

Ecological theory offers a less-biased basis from which to make a social assessment because ecological theory assumes interaction of individuals
and the environment, without specifying either the individual or the environment as standards. Further, the dynamism of the interactions allow for change

without predetermined directions or conclusions. Individuals and environmental behaviors are free to vary their relationships. This framework identifies targets for social work intervention in micro-, macro-, and combined systemic variables.

DETERMINING THE BIAS

As discussed above, "nonbias" is an unreachable goal and the school social worker, in order to maintain an ethical standard, must constantly ask, "How will this assessment affect the client and the environment?" The answers are not always easy. However, the following questions may be used to determine the bias that invariably creeps into assessment.

First, what are the value preferences apparent in the selection of the parts of the ecosystem that are to be assessed? It is obvious that the school social worker, the financial supporters of the social service program, and colleagues or team members have more interest in and concern about some facets of children's problems than others. For example, interests in teenage pregnancy would slant the assessment differently from interests in substance abuse. The biases are better controlled when the preference of the assessor, the agency, and social standards of the environment are openly accepted.

The language chosen in an assessment is another source of bias. This bias might be discovered in the words themselves, in definitions of words, and in appropriate use. For example, "instability" often refers to length of time rather than to the quality of the relationships. "Disorganization" is used to describe any organization other than that which is linear. "Culturally deprived" is used to describe the culturally different. "Marriage" tends to limit itself to the legal and/or social definition at the expense of excluding the emotional definition. By redefining the terms "stable," "organization," "culture," and "marriage," the bias can be identified in words. The assessment instrument which was developed by these authors has words which imply wellness and which individualize functioning.

The second question is, What are the causal agents as seen in an assessment? For example, if a standardized IQ test is used in the assessment of a school child and the IQ score is low, the child's problems in learning are probably perceived as being caused by an inability to learn. Knowing the cultural bias and the questionable reliability of standardized IQ tests, however, it is apparent that the identified cause of the child's difficulty in learning has biased the assessment. In this manner, the perception of cause can be a source of bias in an assessment. The instrument that is presented in this article does not include causation for that reason.

The third question is: Which information is significant in the assessment? Throughout <u>Children of Crisis</u> by Robert Coles, a consistent theme is that the southern black children of this study showed what he thought was amazing strength and fortitude. He quotes a woman who said,

> To me, having a baby inside me is the only time I'm
> really alive. I know I can make something, do something,
> no matter what color my skin is, and what names people call
> me. When the baby gets born I see him, and he's full of
> life, or she is; and I think to myself that it doesn't make
> any difference what happens later, at least now we've got
> a change, or the baby does. 4/

An awareness of the possibility of this attitude is important in assessing
the social situation of a pregnant teenager. The bias is relatively easy
to identify in this example because the prospective mother's attitude varies
from the general societal attitude.

The above three questions may help determine the biases in a social
assessment. The more open the social worker is to admitting biases and
the more skill is used in identifying biases, the more the assessment can
move toward an absence of bias. After raising these questions, it is evident that the practitioner needs a tool that will aid in identifying bias
and reduce it.

THE INSTRUMENT IN THE ASSESSMENT PROCESS

An instrument called Assessment of Child and Adolescent Functioning (ACAF)
has been constructed by the authors. It is designed to meet the following
objectives: (1) identify the degree of fit between a child and the child's
environment, (2) allow professional autonomy and flexibility in selecting
foci of attention, (3) identify positive strengths of clients as opposed to
an excessive preoccupation with pathologies, (4) facilitate clear and understandable goal setting with clients and their parents avoiding technical
language as much as possible, (5) facilitate the mapping of specific social
functioning strengths and weaknesses which affect the individual service
plan and call attention to omissions, and (6) provide measures of functioning which serve as indicators of pre- and post-service progress evaluations.

In developing the instrument, the authors also followed technical criteria for social work instrumentation which make it an efficient and practical tool for daily use in schools and social agencies. It is _comprehensive_,
including forty-six types of social functioning. The types of functioning
are clearly _organized_ for simplicity in recording-keeping and filing. The instrument is _streamlined_ for efficient record-keeping by providing descriptive
statements which are easily marked. In short, paperwork is reduced while
professional flexibility and thoroughness are encouraged in the completion
of an assessment.

Nine general features of social functioning are addressed in the instrument. They result from a review of the parts of the ecosystem addressed
by social workers in practice with children and adolescents. These features
are: coping with problematic behavior, crisis management, adjustment to
disability, family life, sexual growth, school life, neighborhood and community life, care of self, and personal satisfaction. These nine features

110

of social functioning serve to organize the instrument into sections, each of which might be used alone in an assessment or in conjunction with others. The first three sections address immediate problem-solving issues. The next four identify interactions within the child's environment and the last two are personal growth areas. Each section contains within it four to six forms of social functioning which are arranged in an order from "internal" functioning such as self awareness to interpersonal relations and "external" or publicly observable problem-solving behavior. Examples of this continuum are shown in Figure 1.

The ACAF instrument determines the degree to which a person fits the social environment and achieves a balance of selfhood in that situation. Descriptions of four levels are provided for each of the forty-six types of functioning. These descriptive statements aid a practitioner in making an assessment. Levels are standardized for four degrees of fitness: highly acceptable, moderately acceptable, moderately troubled, and severely troubled. To properly assess a client's social functioning, the practitioner must only select the most accurate descriptive statement for each relevant item, perhaps adding a few words of individual detail. The selection is a measure of social functioning.

Finally, the practitioner may use the same set of descriptive statements to set goals and, after a period of service delivery, measure the degree of progress or regression. A goal may be a higher level of functioning or maintenance of an existing level of functioning under anticipated stress. Again, a simple mark on the form indicates a level of functioning achieved. Goals are either "primary" (P) or "secondary" (S) objectives for both the client and practitioner. Another mark on the form indicates the level of functioning after a period of service. Figure 2 demonstrates the efficiency of the instrument for keeping records and standardizing measurements. It should be noted that only careful practitioners make useful and less-biased assessments, using the instrument as a tool which raises the practitioner's consciousness of biased omissions.

The selection of types of functioning and the assessment in the "now" column of Figure 2 indicates a need for some form of intervention. A child whose anxieties prevent normal functioning may need extra supportive attention, rational emotive therapy, and/or activity therapy. Further, it is not necessary for every assessed type of functioning to be "troubled" to benefit from intervention; higher levels of functioning may be desirable in instances of normal functioning to reinforce gains expected in troubled areas.

DEVELOPMENT AND USE OF THE INSTRUMENT

ACAF was developed as an outgrowth of another instrument called Assessment of Adult Social Functioning (AASF) by MacNair, Wodarski, and Giordano. 5/ A succession of field tests was used in refining and simplifying the language as well as streamlining the technical format of the instrument as a practical tool. When a reliability test was finally performed on AASF, it was found to be unreliable when used with adolescent clients but highly

Fig. 1. Illustrated Forms of Social Functioning a/

Crisis Management	Personal Satisfaction

Internal

Emotional clarity in crisis event	Self-acceptance
Control of emotions	Close friendships
Learning from experience	Assertiveness
Coping with loss or separation	Ability to work
Response to new parent figures	Learning outside of school

External

a/ Each form of social functioning is assessed only if it is regarded as relevant.

Fig. 2. Illustration of the Format

Section 2. Crisis Prevention and Management   ☐ Not Applicable

2. Control of Emotions ☐ Not Applicable	Now	Goals		Later
Readily overcomes intense emotions	4	P	S	4
Maintains calm behavior while experiencing intense emotions	3	P	S	3
Allows emotions to reduce essential activities	2	P	S	2
Allows intense emotions to prevent essential activities	1			1

reliable with adults. At that point the authors determined that a more specific child and adolescent instrument, ACAF, was needed. Another review of literature and a series of field tests followed and ACAF was produced. Reliability tests are yet to be performed and the instrument is considered to be in a refined, but preliminary form. Reliability testing may produce further revisions. The format and most of its content will probably remain stable. The design and its utility will remain the same.

ACAF is designed to have a variety of uses. First, it reminds the practitioners of the broad range of social functioning issues which may be pertinent to a case. Practitioners tend to raise certain questions habitually, overlooking problems which may be identified and ignoring certain strengths. The stimulus range of the instrument is its major bias-reducing function. Practitioners should not use the instrument in a mechanical way, however, because it could distract the client. It is advisable to use natural, professional interviewing techniques, giving attention to the client rather than to an instrument. In such interviewing it is vital to refer to a framework of social functioning categories such as ACAF provides.

The instrument is used by the practitioner as a guide in setting goals and identifying points of intervention. Goals are set with clients when possible and they are set at a feasible level. Under conditions of crisis or stress, it is legitimate to set existing levels of functioning as goals, recognizing that behavior may deteriorate under pressure. Practitioners may also use the instrument to evaluate the degree of progress made by clients as a result of intervention and the passage of time. Further, a review of a number of cases will allow the practitioner to see the progress made by a variety of clients. Through such a review, practitioners can analyze the successes and non-successes and styles of intervention associated with them. In other words, they can assess the effectiveness of their own practice. It would be counterproductive to use ACAF to evaluate subordinates. Any hint of punitive applications would destroy the instrument's reliability.

IMPLEMENTATION

To initiate the use of the instrument, it is important to respect the autonomy and professional status of the users. The instrument captures, simplifies, and summarizes highly complex details which could potentially be addressed in the ecological model of human behavior. Practitioners adapt to its use gradually and progressively. Steps in an implementation process are suggested as follows: (1) begin with one or two specialized cases, using one or two sections of the instrument, (2) offer training in the use of the instrument, using a training book and videotape (soon to be made available by the authors), (3) use a participatory decision-making style, asking practitioners to evaluate ACAF's usefulness and making sensible adjustments in procedure, and (4) emphasize the efficiency of record-keeping and the improvement of services to clients; then reward people for increasing thoroughness in its use.

CONCLUSION

This article is an effort to resolve the issue of nonbias in social assessment. A conceptual discussion offers definitions of social assessment, social work assessment, and nonbias. Ecological theory is discussed as the basis for a nonbiased social assessment. Three questions are asked for determining the bias. ACAF serves to implement the ideals of the ecological model in a practical efficient format.

Social workers need an unbiased instrument which reflects concern for professionalism rather than accountability by itself. The instrument serves to guide a process of administering direct services to clients which integrates the need for documentation and accountability with the needs of clients for thorough and carefully planned intervention. The instrument emphasizes strengths of clients. It gives practitioners clear and systematic guides to professional assessment.

NOTES AND REFERENCES

1. Florence Hollis, Casework: A Psychosocial Therapy (New York: Random House, 1964), p. 170.

2. H.C. Cowles, "The Ecological Relations of the Vegetation of the Sand Dunes of Lake Michigan," Botanical Gazette, 27 (1899), pp. 95-117.

3. J.S. Wohlwill, "Behavior Response and Adaptation to Environmental Stimulation," in A. Damon, ed., Physical Anthropology (Cambridge, Mass.: Harvard University Press, 1972).

4. Robert Coles, Children of Crisis (New York: Dell Publishing Co., 1967), p. 368.

5. See Ray H. MacNair, Assessment of Social Functioning: A Client Instrument for Practitioners (Athens: Institute of Community and Area Development, University of Georgia, 1981).

USE OF SELF-CONCEPT MEASURES
AS ASSESSMENT AND ACCOUNTABILITY TOOLS
FOR SCHOOL SOCIAL WORK PRACTICE

RODNEY G. SCHOFIELD

Within the past two years, considerable emphasis has been placed on the need to evaluate the effectiveness of school social work services. 1/ As school social work practitioners find themselves increasingly concerned with accountability there is a need to consider the impact of their interventions on both the cognitive and affective domains of students' school performance.

Encouraging is the fact that leaders in education and school social work are directing the attention of practitioners in their respective fields to the broader, mutual concerns of both professions. For example, Costin has encouraged school social workers to focus on the more traditional educational goals dealing with cognitive processes. 2/ Accordingly, educators are told they must now be concerned with affective educational outcomes in evaluating a total educational program. 3/

RELATIONSHIP BETWEEN SELF-CONCEPT AND ACHIEVEMENT

One area that links the concerns and practices of both social work and education is the relationship between student self-concept and school achievement. Social workers have long been committed to exploring the client's perception of self and environment with emphasis upon the affective determinants of social functioning. Due to new knowledge regarding right hemispheric functioning and the impact of self-perception on learning, educators are turning to evaluative measures of school climate and affective student variables to determine educational outcome. Also encouraging is the common recognition by social workers and educators that interventions in the affective domain must relate to the basic academic goals of the schools.

There is considerable evidence that this relationship does exist when the affective variable is perception of, and feeling about, self. Purkey reviewed the literature pertaining to self-concept and success in school and found "the overwhelming body of contemporary research points insistently to the relationship between self-esteem and academic achievement and suggests strongly that the self-concept can no longer be ignored by parents and teachers." 4/ Support for this conclusion is found in a series of studies which discovered, first, a significant relationship between the individual student's self-concept and the perceptions which he or she felt four others (father, mother, best friend, and teacher) had of him or her. Secondly, longitudinal studies confirmed that students' perceptions of the evaluations of their academic ability by others (teachers, parents, and friends) are associated with self-concepts of that ability. 5/ Since school social work interventions are often directed at enabling parents and teachers to understand and relate to the individual student in ways that enhance that individual's functioning and achievement, the effect of our work on the perceptions and behaviors of parents and teachers as translated into student self-concept would seem an appropriate focus of accountability.

UTILIZATION OF SELF-CONCEPT MEASURES

Self-concept measures can be used to assist school social workers in many areas of practice for purposes of assessment and accountability. First, self-report of student self-esteem can be used along with perceptions of that self-concept by teacher, parent, and social worker to appraise social-emotional functioning. Taken in the context of other indicators of student self-regard, self-concept measures can provide information and baseline data regarding one of the predisposing factors in a student's school and home problems. In the absence of intellectual, sensory, or health factors, a student's inability to learn can often be related to a negative academic self-concept which can be determined, in part, by scores on a self-concept inventory. Conversely, student perceived strengths can often be identified by such measures and used to develop a treatment plan.

Since perceptions of a student's feelings toward self by others is subject to the unique and, at times, distorted "perceptual screen" of the observer, student administered self-concept scales can provide a more accurate, bias-free assessment of self-esteem. With student permission, this assessment can be shared in parent conferences and staffings for the purpose of developing an appropriate educational plan based on specific self-concept needs.

This leads to an area in which self-concept measures can be used as accountability tools in evaluating progress on particular Individualized Educational Plan (IEP) objectives. Since improvement in peer relationships, parent-child relationships, school performance, and personal self-worth are often included in social work developed IEPs, the use of self-concept measures that include the above categories in the report analysis can be helpful in determining changes in student self-concept as a result of social work intervention. 6/ Administration of student self-concept measures on a pre and post basis will provide baseline and after-treatment scores to use in evaluating the effect of individual and group counseling and parent and teacher consultation on student perception of progress on particular affective and social objectives. Comparing individual changes

116

in self-concept scores with that of a control group of students not receiving social work help lends further validity in evaluating social work intervention.

Finally, self-concept measures become valuable research tools in evaluating school social work program effectiveness when control groups and statistical methods are utilized. Since the relationship between student self-concept and academic success has been positively established, evaluation of school social work programs providing direct or indirect service to students could include changes in individual and group self-concept scores as one measure of program effectiveness.

In terms of direct service evaluation, one approach would be to establish experimental and control groups by selecting random samples of students served by school social work who have self-concept related objectives on their IEPs, students served for non self-concept related IEP objectives, and students not receiving school social work service. The next step would involve administering self-concept measures to the groups on a pre, post, and follow-up basis over a period of months and applying an analysis of covariance statistical procedure to the results. The Scheffe test for mutiple comparisons can be used to test for significant differences among the groups. Information obtained through statistical evaluation can then be compared with more subjective data such as questionnaires, interviews, teacher observations, and grades to determine if, in fact, school social work interventions are significant in enhancing student self-concept and improving academic success.

A similar research approach can be used when evaluating indirect services. As indicated in the Brookover study, parents and teachers have the greatest impact on student self-concept. 7/ Therefore, social work program interventions with parent and teacher groups should consider pre and post student self-concept scores as one measure of effectiveness.

For example, parent groups led by school social workers using a variety of program formats are increasingly used as a related support service for handicapped children. One study using the Coopersmith Self-Esteem Inventory and conducted by a school social worker determined that a parent program based on humanistic educational principles was more effective in significantly improving student self-esteem and parent attitudes toward childrearing than a behaviorally oriented program. 8/ This resulted in the author's school district making extensive use of humanistically oriented parent education programs through the school social work delivery system.

Another indirect social work service encouraged by handicapped children's legislation is the provision of staff development and in-service programs for teachers and administrators. Providing educators with knowledge and skills to use in identifying, understanding, and relating to the needs of handicapped children can be expected to eventually impact the self-concept of students. Thus, analysis of pre and post self-concept tests of student groups served by educators who have been in-serviced by social workers can serve to assess this impact.

Recent school social work innovations in using nonhandicapped peers to successfully integrate profoundly handicapped children within the regular school setting has resulted in significantly improved self-esteem among the nonhandicapped students. 9/ The Primary Self-Concept Scale and Coopersmith Self-Esteem Inventory were used to establish this program outcome, which can be used to support the more extensive involvement of nonhandicapped students by social workers in programs for all handicapped students.

In order to insure adequate validity of our efforts to use self-concept measures for evaluation of program effectiveness, it is desirable to enlist the expertise of a research and planning consultant independent of the social work program or department. This will limit the possibility of bias in development of the research design or interpretation of findings.

The use of self-concept measures by school social workers in determining progress on IEP objectives and in assessing program effective-ness has the advantage of placing the focus of evaluation on our efforts rather than on evaluation of the student. This takes into consideration the importance of limiting our attempts at accountability to the variable we can most easily control, that of our own interventions. Bills has expressed his opinion that self-concept measures "should be directed at the quality of our offerings while still remembering that students' learning is not entirely dependent on our effectiveness since it is also dependent on their past experiences and present perceptions." 10/

REPRESENTATIVE SELF-CONCEPT MEASURES

While there are many self-concept instruments available, a few have appeared sufficiently in the research literature to warrant consideration by social work practitioners and researchers. For the purpose of describing typical self-concept measures for use by school social workers, the author has selected three instruments which have established adequate validity and reliability, have been designed for application with students at distinct age groupings, and are in use by the author's school social work department.

Primary Self-Concept Inventory (PSCI). 11/ This test was designed to identify students with undesirably low self-concepts and has the advantage of being constructed for successful application with multi-cultural groups. The inventory is especially applicable with primary age children, does not require that the child be able to read, and can be administered in any language or combination of languages. The PSCI is composed of twenty items which measure six aspects or factors of self-concept that can be clustered into three major domains: personal-self, social-self, and intellectual-self. When used as a beginning screening device the PSCI can be especially helpful in the social work assessment process and in evaluating progress on self-concept-related IEP objectives. One aspect of the PSCI that may limit its validity over the next decade is its use of some stereotypical sex-based role behaviors in the test booklets developed for girls and boys.

Coopersmith Self-Esteem Inventory (CSEI). 12/ This fifty-item scale was developed to measure self-esteem of children ages 8 to 12, although it has been used with age ranges from 8 to adult in separate forms. The inventory measures evaluative attitudes toward the self in social, academic, family and personal areas of experience. There is also a lie scale to assess extremely socialized response sets. The CSEI has been widely used by researchers over the past ten years and established impressive reliability and validity. The inventory form has the advantage of being self-administered and takes about ten minutes to complete. Due to its relatively nonthreatening format, the CSEI lends itself to discussion between social worker and student and/or parent as to identified areas of concern.

Tennessee Self-Concept Scale (TSCS). 13/ The TSCS consists of one hundred self-descriptive statements which students repond to on a five-point scale from completely false to completely true. It is written for ages 12 and higher and can be used with the whole range of students from healthy to severely emotionally disturbed. The TSCS has two forms, the counseling form and the clinical or research form. The counseling form is quicker and easier to score because it deals with fewer variables and scores and is more appropriate for self-interpretation or direct feedback to the student by the social worker. The clinical form is more appropriate for use and interpretation by the school psychologist.

The TSCS provides a number of scores which produce a multidimensional self-concept profile of the student. A self-criticism score is used to determine the degree of defensiveness and validity of the student's responses. The total positive (P) score reflects the overall level of student self-esteem and comprises the following separate categories of self-concept: identity, self-satisfaction, behavior, physical self, moral-ethical self, personal self, family self, and social self. Plotting the separate categorical scores on the profile sheet allows students to quickly identify areas of their life that tend to diminish their self-esteem. The author has found secondary students especially interested in subsequent retests on the TSCS to affirm their growth in positive self-concept. Validity and reliability studies for the TSCS are comparable to, or exceed, similar self-concept measures.

The above self-concept tests are representative, but not necessarily superior to, other instruments developed for the purpose of measuring the affective variable of student self-esteem. The Primary Self-Concept Inventory, Coopersmith Self-Esteem Inventory, and Tennessee Self-Concept Scale have been selected for discussion in this paper because they are appropriate for different age groupings and have been widely used by the author's school social work department for assessment and program evaluation.

SPECIAL CONSIDERATIONS

While using self-concept tests for the purposes outlined in this paper, it is important to keep in mind that such measures are but one of many approaches to assessing the affective domain of children. Leonetti cautions that no single assessment instrument should be used as the total criterion for evaluating the cognitive or affective domains of a student. 14/ This procedural safeguard is written into current handicapped children's legislation which requires a minimum of two independent assessments in determining the presence of a handicap, including affective disturbances.

School social workers have many techniques at their disposal for assessing the self-esteem of students. These include individual and group sessions with students and parents, use of the social-developmental history, teacher consultation, role plays, sociograms, and school climate appraisal. Most importantly, the establishment of an empathic, accepting relationship with a student and his or her family can provide more basic information about the self-worth of a student than any objective test. The establishment of such a relationship should be the primary assessment and, certainly, treatment technique of the school social work practitioner.

The process of incorporating self-concept testing into a school social work department's assessment and accountability procedures should involve consultation with the school district's school psychology department. This will reduce possible concern by psychologists that social workers are operating in an area for which they are not equipped. When social workers point out their involvement with the affective domain of students and demonstrate an appreciation of the limitations of objective tests used in isolation of other data, such professional rivalry need not occur. In fact, school psychologists can be helpful in assessing the validity and appropriateness of certain self-concept measures as well as aiding in their interpretation.

SUMMARY

The ancient Chinese sages used the analogy of the praying mantis who tried to stop a carriage by raising his front legs to define self-confidence. (The Japanese philosophers saw this as a symbol of valor beyond reason.) Our current knowledge of perceptual psychology has defined more specifically the essence of self-concept and has developed behaviorally objective tools to supplement our clinical evaluation of an individual's self-esteem. These tools or self-concept measures become valuable adjuncts to school social work's efforts to improve assessment and accountability procedures when we consider the relationship between the cognitive and affective domains in the learning process.

Research evidence has shown a clear and strong relationship between positive self-concept and academic success, and negative self-concept and school failure. The presence and development of a positive self-concept is considered a necessary, although not sufficient, condition for student scholastic achievement. Since much of a school social worker's intervention relates to the development of positive student self-concept, measures of this affective variable become an effective and valid tool for evaluating school social work service as it relates to school achievement.

NOTES AND REFERENCES

1. See "Special Issue on Evaluating Practice," Social Work in Education (entire issue), 2 (April 1980); Norma Radin, "Assessing the Effectiveness of School Social Workers," Social Work, 24 (March 1979), pp. 132-137; and Arthur P. Michals, David E. Cournoyer, and Elizabeth L. Pinner, "School Social Work and Educational Goals," Social Work, 24 (March 1979), pp. 138-143.

2. Lela B. Costin, "Social Work Contribution to Education in Transition," in Rosemary C. Sarri and Frank F. Maple, eds., The School in the Community (Washington, D.C.: National Association of Social Workers, 1972), p. 36.

3. See Robert E. Bills, "Affect and its Measurement," in William J. Gephart, Robert B. Ingle, and Frederick J. Marshall, eds., Evaluation in the Affective Domain (Bloomington, Ind.: Phi Delta Kappa, 1976), pp. 7-52.

4. William Purkey, Self Concept and School Achievement (Englewood Cliffs, N.J.: Prentice Hall, 1970), pp. v-vi.

5. Wilbur Brookover, Edsel Erickson, and L. Joiner, Self-Concept of Ability and School Achievement, Vol. 3: Relationship of Self-Concept to Achievement in High School (East Lansing, Mich.: Michigan State University, 1967).

6. See Jean Campbell, "Individualized Educational Programs as a Tool in Evaluation," Social Work in Education, 2 (April 1980), pp. 19-24.

7. See Brookover, Erickson, and Joiner, op. cit.

8. See Rod Schofield, "Parent Group Education and Student Self-Esteem," Social Work in Education, 1 (January 1979), pp. 26-33.

9. See Joe Gianesin, "Steps and Processes of Successfully Integrating the Profoundly Handicapped Child Within a Regular School Setting." Unpublished manuscript, Colorado Springs (Colorado) Public Schools, 1981.

10. Bills, op. cit., p. 26.

11. See Douglas G. Muller and Robert Leonetti, Primary Self-Concept Inventory Test Manual (Boston, Mass.: Teaching Resources Corp., 1974).

12. See Stanley Coopersmith, The Antecedents of Self-Esteem (San Francisco: W.H. Freeman & Co., 1967).

13. William H. Fitts, Tennessee Self Concept Scale Manual (Nashville, Tenn.: Counselor Recordings and Tests, 1965).

14. Robert Leonetti, Self Concept and the School Child: How to Enhance Self-Confidence and Self-Esteem (New York: Philosophical Library, 1980), p. 45.

SYSTEMS MODEL OF SCHOOL SOCIAL WORK: BARRIERS TO IMPLEMENTATION

Terry Zielinski and Julie Coolidge

This article will review the development of the systems model of school social work and the barriers to implementing such a model. The research was undertaken in a ten-school rural special education cooperative. Particular attention is paid to the role of the traditional approach to school social work. The authors theorized that the first line of resistance, if any, to implementing a systems model of school social work would be the school administrators who use the social worker's services. As a result, the authors have concentrated their research efforts on administrative attitudes toward a systems approach versus a traditional approach.

HISTORICAL REVIEW

In the United States, school social work had its origins in 1906. 1/ School social work was primarily funded through the efforts of private agencies. School social work represented a response to

> certain specific influences--the passage of compulsory
> school attendance law, new knowledge about individual
> differences among children and their capacities to re-
> spond to improved conditions, and the realization of
> the strategic place of school and education in the lives
> of children and youths coupled with concerns for the
> relevance of education to the child's present and
> future. 2/

During the first thirty years of school social work's development, the role of the school social worker, generally stated, was to be a home-school-community liaison. 3/ However, the population to be served did not change appreciably until the 1970s. Generally, school attendance problems were and still are a major focus of the school social worker. 4/ Also, children with a variety of problems adjusting to the school setting were considered problems to be addressed by the school social worker. 5/ Generally speaking, the school social worker, in his or her role as a home-school-community liaison would attempt to organize the resources of the home, school, and community in order to bring these resources to bear on the specific problems of a student.

This method underwent dramatic changes in the 1920s and 1930s, due primarily to the mental hygiene movement of that time. The most important change was that "school social workers began to turn more attention to work with the individual maladjusted child at school, in addition to their traditional work with others in the child's behalf--at home, in school, and in the community." 6/

The emphasis on the child's maladjustment to the school setting continued until the 1960s. The civil strife of the 1960s seemed to have an impact on all areas of social work, including school social work. During this period of time

> school social work literature began to urge a transition to new goals and methods of work and to reflect a new awareness of the school as a social system and a greater readiness of the professions of education and social work to collaborate . . . . There was a renewed focus on school social work's responsibility to help modify school conditions and policies that were obstacles to successful school experience for children. 7/

CURRENT VIEWS OF SCHOOL SOCIAL WORK

In 1969, Costin presented major findings in her analysis of school social work tasks. She found that

> professionals were relying on a definition of their work that was focused primarily on casework with the individual child, dealing with his emotional problems and his personal adjustment. The problems of the child in school were viewed as arising mostly from his personal characteristics or those of his parents. The impact that school policies and community conditions had on pupils had gone almost unrecognized. School social workers had minimized the importance of their responsibilities for leadership in modifying school and community conditions. 8/

Costin concluded that school social workers were not attuned to the urgent problems of children and youth.

Gottlieb and Gottlieb's analysis of the traditional social work model in schools lead them to conclude, as Costin did, that the traditional model is insufficient for school social work today. 9/ The Gottliebs contend that school social workers must become more knowledgeable in their ability to assess systemwide problems in the schools. 10/ The authors contend that social workers are not trained to do such assessment: "He [the social worker] is not oriented toward effecting systemic changes in the factors that cause individual maladjustment. Nor does his educational background encourage competence in primary prevention activities: early casefinding, developing new resources for the school, and discussing policy formulation with administrators." 11/

124

The Gottlieb analysis, although excellent in terms of explaining why school social workers have few skills to implement a systems model, offers no model for a systems model of school social work.

In 1971, Alderson and Krishef used Costin's measurements in order to make an analysis of the tasks of school social workers in Florida. This study was done five years after Costin's original study. Perhaps due to the impact of Costin's study in 1968, the Florida study found that school social workers rated leadership and policymaking highest and casework with individual children lowest. 12/ This turnabout in social worker attitudes is remarkable. However, this study, while supporting the concept of a systems intervention approach, did not offer a general model of systems intervention.

Another relevant study regarding school social work tasks found agreement between school social workers and principals about a variety of tasks. 13/ In this study, Williams found significant agreement between social workers and principals on the need for school social workers to advise parents about community agencies, inform the principal regarding individual case progress, participation in professional meetings, and investigation of the neighborhood environment. The importance of this study is that it addressed not only school social workers' attitudes towards their tasks, but also principals' attitudes towards these tasks.

In a related study done in Grand Rapids, Michigan, in 1970, there was support for the Williams research cited above. 14/ However, this study went further in terms of a systems model of school social work. The Grand Rapids study found little agreement between school social workers and principals on tasks related to systems intervention. For example, there was little agreement between teachers and principals on changing those systems in which the principal or teacher is the focus of change. In this case, the school social workers were in favor of the systems intervention tasks, but the school principals were not. This study gives the first insights into role expectation problems in implementing a systems intervention model of school social work.

The most comprehensive study of school social worker tasks and how they relate to educational professionals seems to be Flynn's study in 1976. 15/ Flynn compared school social workers' ratings of various tasks with a variety of other educational professionals' ratings of the same tasks, including administrators. His conclusions provide some insight into the systems intervention model of school social work. Flynn concluded that there was a high degree of incongruence in perceptions among and between the various groups measured. While school social workers rated

> broader system and policy interventions significantly
> higher than all other groups . . . they nevertheless
> ranked such orientations lowest among their own pri-
> orities. Yet it is frequently alleged that social
> work interventions beyond the level of individual child
> control are stifled or thwarted by the school system

itself. On the contrary, these findings suggest that
the very ranking of priorities by social workers themselves are a barrier to broader system intervention. 16/

This incongruity suggests that even though school social workers place
a high value on a systems intervention model of school social work, they do
not put priority on such tasks. Perhaps one reason is that there have been
very few models of such a system. It could also mean that school social
workers find that systems intervention is less effective than traditional
forms of intervention. In any event, Flynn did not attempt to elaborate
systems intervention tasks, other than defining them in the broadest terms.
Again, there is no specific model of a systems intervention model offered.

COSTIN'S SYSTEMS MODEL

In 1975, Costin offered the first comprehensive model of a systems approach
to school social work. 17/ She presented not only a general model of a
systems approach to school social work, but also supported the model with
supporting theories from the social sciences. Costin supported her systems
approach to school social work by citing social learning theory and general
systems theory. In regards to social learning theory, she stated:

> Social work practice focusing on school-community-pupil
> relations relies on certain principles of social learn-
> ing. These emphasize the role of social variables as a
> way to account for the development and modification of
> human behavior. Among the specific areas related to the
> pupil's behavior are (1) imitative learning from models,
> (2) the demands and constraints of roles, and (3) the
> influence of cultures. The focus is on learned, overt,
> readily observed maladaptive behavior. 18/

Costin blends general systems theory and social learning theory to offer a
systems model for school social work. Briefly, she described the model as
follows.

> This model, then, emphasizes the links and interactions
> between pupil characteristics and school-community condi-
> tions and practices . . . . Within such a framework, so-
> cial workers respond to identified group patterns of
> underachievement, truancy, absenteeism, exclusion from
> school, or other recurring evidence that schools are
> failing to meet the educational needs of large numbers
> of pupils. The focus on patterns of group behavior does
> not imply that the individual is unimportant. It does
> imply that attention cannot be limited to the individual
> as it points up this fact: The interrelationship of pu-
> pil problems and school-community problems requires deal-
> ing with the problem complex and its network of problem
> situations. 19/

Based on this general model, Costin goes on to illustrate more specific steps in the systems approach to school problems. She states that the first step in solving a problem faced by a school social worker is assessment. However,

> traditional school social work practice generally relies
> on study and evaluation of psychosocial factors that pre-
> vent a child from adjusting to school. Evaluation in-
> cludes personal characteristics, attitudes and behaviors
> of the child who has been referred, interpersonal prob-
> lems within the family, and reports by teachers and
> other specialists. 20/

In contrast, the systems model of school social work would view and natural-
ly assess a problem in a manner far different from the traditional approach
mentioned above. Assessment in a systems framework "relies primarily on
the study and evaluation of how pupil characteristics interact with school-
community conditions and how they affect educational opportunity for groups
of pupils." 21/

In explaining and contrasting the two different approaches to assessing a problem in the school setting, Costin clearly illustrates the emphasis
of the systems approach. It is clear that the systems school social worker
deals primarily with groups and not individuals. The difference is even
more apparent in the service plan of the traditional and systems school social worker. The traditional service plan, according to Costin, is determined primarily by those who refer children; for example, teachers, principals, social agencies, and even parents. 22/ However, the systems model social worker develops "a service plan only after the foregoing procedures of
assessment have been carried out. Then, during continued consultation with
administrators, teachers, and other school personnel," the social worker develops, writes, and offers a plan to administrators and others whose support
is essential. 23/ The plan offered will be directed at solving certain
"problem complexes" by making appropriate changes in elements of the school
system, or even of the broader social system, that seem to be maintaining
the problem complex. 24/ A problem complex, according to Costin, is a
group of interrelated problems that seem to be caused by or maintained by
the school system. 25/

A practical example of the traditional versus systems school social
work approaches can be seen in the problem of attendance. The traditional
worker would receive a referral of a student who is an attendance problem.
The worker would consult the student's individual records, teachers, principal, and other relevant staff. Next, the social worker would contact the
student's family and evaluate their role in the student's attendance. Finally, based on the information secured, the traditional worker would develop a service plan directed at increasing the attendance of the student.

The systems school social worker on the other hand would attempt to
evaluate any patterns within the overall attendance picture. What characteristics exist of children we describe as having attendance problems? Are

there any discernible patterns? Once these questions are answered, the systems worker would develop a service plan that would be directed at altering the specific systemic constraints to student attendance and to developing systemwide behaviors directed at improving and maintaining student attendance.

This review of the literature has illustrated the development of school social work into its present traditional form. Also, this literature review has attempted to illustrate the service challenge posed by the advocates of the systems model of school social work. The next section of this report will examine the practicality of the systems model, the author's conceptualization of how the systems model will look, and the barriers to implementing such a model.

PROCEDURE

The main question is whether school administrators would find a systems approach to school social work acceptable. Would these administrators view such a model in a way that would allow them to approve implementation of the systems approach? One way to answer this question would be to develop a total systems approach and allow school administrators to respond to the model. The authors developed a survey for this purpose. The survey was developed for the Todd-Ottertail-Wadena (TOW) Special Education Cooperative, a ten-school district rural special education cooperative serving approximately 8,900 total student population. The TOW cooperative has had social work services since it began in 1968. The TOW social workers have followed the traditional model, and they provide service not only to students who are identified as handicapped but also serve a large population of students that have attendance and behavioral problems. The following is a summary of the procedures the authors followed in securing data on administrative attitudes toward the systems model of school social work.

INSTRUMENT

The authors wanted to develop a tool that would survey administrator attitudes toward a systems model as compared to a traditional model of school social work. Costin's conceptualization of a systems model was followed as closely as possible. Four distinct problem categories were identified: (1) behavior problems, (2) attendance problems, (3) child abuse and neglect problems, and (4) handicapped children and their problems. Using a job description format, several objectives were written for each of the problem areas, one set for the systems model and one set for the traditional model. First, the administrators were asked to rate their choice of the overall model for each problem area. Second, the administrators were asked to rate each model by choosing a certain number of objectives equal to approximately half of the objectives under the problem category. The reason for choosing only half was to simulate the real constraint of time on the school social worker. In other words, the authors were concerned that the administrators might find both the traditional and systems models attractive.

However, it is unrealistic to think that both systems could be implemented at the same time, given staff time constraints.

The survey form, presented in its entirety in Appendix 1, was sent to all thirty-five administrators in the special education cooperative, including superintendents, principals, and assistant principals. A second mailing was sent after seven days. Administrators were encouraged to contact the authors if they had any questions. After the second mailing, the authors waited seven more days and concluded collecting data. The total number of survey forms completed was thirty.

RESULTS

Column A in the survey represents the traditional model of school social work and Column B represents the systems model of school social work. Of the thirty respondents, the total of Column A selected was 111 ($\leq$CA) as opposed to Column B which had only 9 ($\leq$CB). The same relationship was apparent in selecting individual objectives on tasks in each column. Column A (traditional) tasks were selected a total of 506 ($\leq$TA) times as opposed to Column B tasks (systems) which were chosen only 72 ($\leq$TB) times.

The Kolmogorov-Smirnov one-sample test was employed to test the hypothesis that A is identical in all five possible categories, that is 0 percent, 25 percent, 50 percent, 75 percent, and 100 percent or 6/30. 26/ The critical value in this case is 0.24. Tables 1 and 2 explain the data and computations.

Table 1

Percentage Selecting A	f	f/N Relative Frequency	$Sn(x)$ Cumulative Relative Frequency
0% of Model A	0	0/30	0/30
25% of Model A	0	0/30	0/30
50% of Model A	2	2/30	2/30
75% of Model A	5	5/30	7/30
100% of Model A	23	23/30	30/30

DISCUSSION

The results of this study must be viewed in perspective. It must be kept in mind that the administrators studied have had almost twelve years of experience with a traditional model. However, the results, which tend to support the traditional model overwhelmingly, is suggestive of the administrators' view of the effectiveness of the traditional model, at least in terms of meeting their needs.

In their written comments and in conversations with the authors, the the administrators indicated they saw real value in the systems model.

Table 2

Category	$F_o(x)$	$S_n(x)$	$F_o(x) - S_n(x)$
0% of A	6/30	0/30	6/30
25% of A	12/30	0/30	12/30
50% of A	18/30	2/30	16/30
75% of A	24/30	7/30	17/30 a/
100% of A	30/30	30/30	0/30

a/ Based on a 0.05 level of significance, the critical value equals 0.24. In the case of the data at hand $\underline{D}$ = 17/30 or 0.57, well above the 0.24 level needed to reject the null hypothesis.

However, it seemed that their main concern was that with a systems model, the social worker would have no time to work on individual cases. The administrators recognized the preventive value of the systems model, but reasoned that it would take a great deal of time to realize the benefits of the preventive work. In the meantime, the administrator would have to deal with various individual problems without the help of the social worker. They view the traditional approach as an effective tool in solving individual problems of school children.

It is for these reasons that the administrators are not willing or ready to adopt a systems approach to school social work. This research is also suggestive of a more difficult barrier to a system approach. It seems that as long as administrators view the traditional model as effective, they will resist any changes, given staff time constraints.

NOTES AND REFERENCES

1. Lela B. Costin, "School Social Work," Encyclopedia of Social Work, Vol 1 (17th issue; Washington, D.C.: National Association of Social Workers, 1977), p. 1240.

2. Ibid.

3. Ibid.

4. Ibid.

5. Ibid.

6. Ibid.

7. Ibid.

8. Lela B. Costin, "An Analysis of the Tasks in School Social Work," Social Service Review, 43 (September 1969), pp. 274-285.

9. Benjamin H. Gottlieb and Lois J. Gottlieb, "An Expanded Role for the School Social Worker," Social Work, 16 (October 1971), pp. 12-21.

10. Ibid.

11. Ibid.

12. John J. Alderson and Curtis H. Krishef, "Another Perspective on Tasks in School Social Work," Social Casework, 59 (December 1973), pp. 591-600.

13. Robert B. Williams, "School Compatibility and Social Work Roles," Social Service Review, 44 (June 1970), pp. 169-176.

14. "Social Service Delivery for Multi-Problem Families in the Grand Rapids Public Schools," Western Michigan University School of Social Work, Kalamazoo, 1970. Mimeographed.

15. John P. Flynn, "Congruence in Perception of Social Work--Related Tasks in a School System," Social Service Review, 50 (September 1976), pp. 471-481.

16. Ibid.

17. Lela B. Costin, "School Social Work Practice: A New Model," Social Work, 20 (March 1975), pp. 135-139.

18. Ibid., p. 136.

19. Ibid.

20. Ibid., p. 137.

21. Ibid.

22. Ibid.

23. Ibid., p. 138.

24. Ibid.

25. Ibid.

26. Lyman Ott et al., Statistics: A Tool for the Social Sciences (2d ed; North Scituate, Mass.: Duxbury Press, 1978), p. 251.

Appendix A. The Survey Instrument.

Instructions

This survey is directed at evaluating school administrator attitudes toward different models of school social work. In this survey, you will find four problem areas usually dealt with by school social workers. They are attendance problems, behavior problems, child abuse and neglect, and children who receive special education services. You will find two columns under each of these categories (Column A and B). Each column represents a unique group of tasks that the social worker could perform in your school.

First, place an X in the box next to the column of tasks you prefer your school social worker to perform in dealing with the specific problem area. You may pick only one column. You are asked to make this choice for each of the four problem categories.

Second, you will notice a line next to each objective in both columns. Please put an X on the lines next to the individual objectives you prefer. You may choose objectives from either column. However, you may not exceed the number indicated at the top of the column.

Respondent Information

What is your present position?

High School	Elem. School	Principal	Assistant to Principal	Superintendent

Years in the above position? _____

Years of experience you have had using a school social worker? _____

Sex _____

Age _____

First, choose one column for a child who has been identified as having a behavior problem.

Second, put an X on the lines that indicate your preference for individual objectives. You may choose from either column A or B. For this problem area you may choose four (4) objectives.

132

COLUMN A	COLUMN B

COLUMN A   ☐

COLUMN B   ☐

___1. The social worker will accept referral on individual cases of children with behavior problems.

___2. The social worker will work with the child's family in order to secure the family's cooperation in solving the specific behavior problem.

___3. The social worker will evaluate the family's capacity to help the school solve the specific behavior problem.

___4. The social worker will make recommendations to the administrator, directed at implementing a specific program to solve the behavior problem. This may include behavior modification programs, or individual or group counseling, or specific counseling for the family.

___5. The social worker will work closely with other public or private agencies in an effort to coordinate these outside resources in solving the child's behavior problem.

___1. The social worker will coordinate efforts of the administrators and other school staff in evaluating current school policies and practices that promote or inhibit prosocial behavior.

___2. The social worker will make recommendations to the school administration regarding school policy and procedure changes directed at increasing prosocial behavior of students.

___3. The school social worker will develop, coordinate, and implement a series of parent-training programs directed at improving the parents' capacity to manage their children effectively. These training sessions will be directed at helping parents improve homework behavior, social behaviors in the classroom, and assignment-completion behaviors of their children.

First, choose one column for students who are attendance problems.

Second, put an X on the lines that indicate your preference for individual objectives. You may choose from either Column A or B. For this problem area you may choose five (5) objectives.

COLUMN A   ☐

COLUMN B   ☐

___1. Refer individual cases to the social worker as you determine a need.

___2. The social worker will work with the family and student in order to increase attendance.

___3. The social worker will report back to the principal on the progress of the case.

___4. The social worker will make recommendations and take steps to implement individual programs designed to increase attendance such as behavior management or referral to public social service agencies.

___5. The social worker will work with other staff, i.e. counselors, special educators, etc. in order to increase the individual student's attendance.

___1. The social worker will work with the principal and other appropriate administrators to evaluate the effectiveness of current school attendance policies.

___2. The social worker, with the cooperation of the school administration will evaluate current school policies and practices that might indirectly affect (positive/negative) student attendance.

___3. The social worker, in cooperation with the school administration will identify student attitude and behaviors that contribute to or inhibit proper attendance.

___4. The social worker will make recommendations to the school administration regarding policy and procedure changes that would improve school attendance.

___5. The social worker will take part in implementing policy and procedural changes directed at improving overall student attendance.

First, choose one column for students who are known or suspected to be abused or neglected.

Second, put an X on the lines that indicate your preference for individual objectives. You may choose from either Column A or B. For this problem area you may only choose five (5) objectives.

COLUMN A

COLUMN B

___1. The school social worker will accept individual referrals of children who are suspected to be abused.

___1. The school social worker will coordinate, develop, and implement in-service training for teachers that is directed at improving the teacher's

___2. The social worker will work closely with the county social welfare agency responsible for accepting abuse/neglect reports.

___3. In each individual case, the social worker will provide services to the family that are directed at improving the family's capacity to parent their child.

___4. The social worker will provide individual services to the child who is a victim of abuse. These may include individual or group counseling to reverse the effect of abuse or neglect on the child.

___5. The social worker will provide special services, in conjunction with mental health and social welfare agencies, directed at children who have been sexually abused. These services may include age-appropriate treatment regarding the sexual abuse victim's self-esteem.

___6. The school social worker will participate on the local community child protection team.

skills in identification and reporting of child abuse.

___2. The school social worker will coordinate, develop, and implement a series of parent-training programs directed at improving child management and communication skills for parents that are identified as high risk to abuse or neglect their children.

___3. The school social worker will develop and implement special parenting classes for those parents who are high-risk parents that are illiterate or mentally handicapped.

___4. The school social worker, in coordination with school administration, will develop and implement school policies regarding child abuse. This will include developing a written policy for identification and reporting of child abuse.

___5. The school social worker, in coordination with school administration will develop curriculum directed at prevention of child abuse, sexual abuse, and neglect. This may include curriculum development such as decision making for marriage, parenting, and sexuality and sexual abuse awareness.

First, choose one column for a child who presents specific problems due to a handicapping condition such as mental retardation, physical handicaps, learning disabilities, speech, hearing, vision impairment, etc.

Second, put an X on the lines that indicate your preference for individual objectives. You may choose from either Column A or B. For this problem area you may only choose six (6) objectives.

COLUMN A a/   COLUMN B

[ ]   [ ]

___1. The social worker will accept   ___1. The school social worker will
referrals on individual prob-   cooperate with special educa-
lems of students who are   tors, administrators, and
handicapped.   parent advocacy groups in
                                         evaluating local school
___2. The social worker will pro-   policies that might promote
vide counseling individually,   or inhibit the effectiveness
or in groups, to parents and   of special educational pro-
students regarding the unique   grams.
social, emotional, educational,
and vocational problems asso-   ___2. The school social worker will
ciated with handicapping   coordinate and cooperate with
conditions.   administrators in evaluating
                                         the impact of specific school
___3. The social worker will identi-   policies that are directed
fy service and resources in   toward mainstream education
the community that are appro-   but that might have a negative
priate to the special needs   impact on the handicapped
of the handicapped student.   student.

___4. The social worker will parti- ___3. The school social worker will
cipate in individual educa-   coordinate, develop, and im-
tional program conferences at   plement a curriculum program
the invitation of the special   (K-12) directed at increasing
education staff and school   understanding and acceptance
administration. In this   of handicapped students by
capacity the social worker   mainstream students.
will assist in the develop-
ment of individualized edu-   ___4. The social worker will coordi-
cational programs where   nate, develop, and implement
appropriate.   a program directed at minimiz-
                                         ing the effects of the intense
___5. The social worker will help   psychological adjustment and
ensure full participation of   emotional isolation that many
individual parents in the   parents of newborn severely
entire special education   handicapped children initial-
process, from evaluation to   ly experience. This might in-
program development, by ex-   clude a program of utilizing
plaining the rights of chil-   and training parents of se-
dren and parents to an ap-   verely handicapped children
propriate special education.   who have successfully adjusted
This can be accomplished by   and who are willing to volun-
home visits, telephone con-   teer their time to make regu-
tacts or other means.   lar visits and provide some

_____

a/ Most of these job tasks were adopted from Robert C. Crouch, "Job
Description:School Social Worker (Special Education," _Social Work in Educa-_
tion, 3 (January 1981), pp. 59-61.

136

___6. The social worker will help parents who are culturally different or mentally handicapped, understand the special educational process when normal staff communication does not achieve this goal.

___7. The social worker will serve as a liaison between the school, home, and outside public and private agencies in order to coordinate the efficient delivery of services to maximize the student's special educational program.

emotional support to parents of newborn handicapped children.

___5. The school social worker will coordinate, develop, and implement a series of parent training programs directed at informing parents on a variety of issues of importance such as future planning for their child, medical, legal, recreational and social services available to the handicapped, supplemental security income, etc.

AN OUTCOME FOCUS FOR DIFFERENTIAL
LEVELS OF SCHOOL SOCIAL WORK PRACTICE

Marjorie McQueen Monkman

Social work is concerned with what will happen to individual and environment as a result of the activity which occurs between them. Thus, social
work's outcome measures are changes in people and changes in the capacities
of the environment to nurture and enhance growth in people. The development of this perspective, the explication of outcome measures, and the use
of outcome measures in developing differential levels of school social work
practice will be examined in this article and integrated to form a model
for differential levels of school social work practice.

From the beginning, social work has been concerned with the person-in-
situation complex, a concern that shows social work to have a broader and
more balanced view than most other disciplines. Yet social workers have not
viewed their area of central concern in a manner that enables them to build
knowledge and practice techniques clearly related to their area of central
concern. Recent literature, however, increasingly identifies the area of
central concern to social work as the "betweenness" of "interface" of the
person and the environment. 1/

A major reason for the profession's failure to develop such knowledge
may have been that its language for describing the area of central concern
has not lent itself to knowledge building and the development of practice
principles. Gordon has developed a framework that makes it easier to oper-
ationalize and to capture the uniqueness of the social work focus for practice. 2/ The focus of his framework is the point of direct contact of person and environment: the interface between the individual and whatever
confronts him or her in living.

GORDON'S MODEL

Gordon has referred to this interface as the transactions occurring between
the individual and the environment. He has defined transaction as exchange
in the context of action or activity. This action or activity is a combination of a person's activity and impinging environment activity; thus, exchange occurs only in the context of activity involving both person and environment. The exchanges are created by the individual's coping behavior
on the one hand and the activity of the impinging environment on the
other. 3/

Coping behavior is "that behavior at the surface of the human organism which is capable of being consciously directed toward the management of transaction." 4/ Coping behavior excludes the many activities that are governed by cognitive processes below the conscious level but includes those behaviors that may be directed to the impinging environment and which potentially can be brought under conscious control. The other side of the transaction area is the environment. As a way of partializing, Gordon has defined the qualities of the impinging environment as those qualities at the surface of the environment system with which the person is actually in contact, rather than "below-the-surface" structures that are inferred to be responsible for the nature of what the human organism actually confronts. 5/ In practice, social work has not confined its concern to the person in any particular situation, that is, at home, at the hospital, in school, or in any particular situation. As Gordon has pointed out, no other profession seems to follow humans so extensively into their daily habitat.

The social work practice target is matching, an effort to see "that the environment directed behavior (coping) and the environment originating action (quality of the impinging environment) are such that appropriate exchanges take place." 6/ Matching the coping and the quality means bringing about a fit which makes for positive results for the person and the environment.

Relationship to Theory

Gordon has suggested that this framework for the professional technology of social work may be tied to the second law of thermodynamics. The law generalizes the tendency for unattended systems to move toward disorder rather than order, disorganization rather than organization--in other words, to increase in entropy. Growth and development exhibit essentially opposite trends: a decrease in entropy. Gordon has further explained:

> Organisms are systems of markedly lower entropy than their impinging environment. The achievement (growth and development) of these low entropy systems and their maintenance are critically dependent upon the performance of the transaction intersystem at the organism-environment interface. For growth and development to occur, the transaction intersystem must accomplish a substantial redistribution of entropy between the organism and environment systems. On the organism side, entropy must be rather continuously reduced or be extracted. For the environment to be preserved or ameliorated, the extracted entropy from the organism side must be deployed in such a way that the entropy level of the impinging environment is not itself increased. 7/

This framework represents an ecological perspective or metaphor; ecology seeks to understand the reciprocal relation between organisms and environment: how organisms shape the environment to their needs and how this shaping enhances the life-supporting properties of the environment. 8/ For social work, the ecological perspective is the one that seems to have been adopted in past decades.

One of the reasons for the better fit of the ecological metaphor to social work is that it is a multicausal rather than a linear-causal perspective. That is, attention is called to the consequences of transactions rather than the causes of activity. Traditionally, social workers have been more concerned about consequences of the transactions between people and environment, but the metaphors, models, and theories that have been borrowed have focused more on cause of action.

As the profession's theoretical relationships become clearer, so do its outcome measures. Social work's theoretical orientation, simply stated, is that appropriate intervention can accomplish substantial redistribution of entropy for person and environment. Thus, outcome measures are changes in some part of the coping behaviors and the quality of the impinging environment.

Expanding Gordon's Framework

People cope with themselves or act in relationship to themselves, as well as in relationship to input from the environment. 9/ Often the coping behaviors emitted by an individual or group of individuals are related to the information they have about themselves or their environment. This information may be directing the coping behaviors and may be directing the perception of the environment in a manner that makes it difficult to receive the output or feedback from the environment. If the quality of the impinging environment seems appropriate and not in keeping with the coping behaviors, it is important to reevaluate the information and perceptions of the coping person or persons. This assessment, however, is made from the pattern of coping behaviors, rather than from inferences about the causes of behavior.

Outcome categories. Social work is concerned with what will happen to the coping behaviors and the quality of the impinging environment as a result of the exchanges that occur between them. Thus, coping behaviors and quality of impinging environment become the dependent, or outcome, variables. The exchange "between" or the activity at the "interface" of coping behavior and quality of impinging environment is the independent variable. In other words, the intervention focus, or the independent variable, is some part of the input to the transaction. The social worker may manipulate some input from the coping behavior side or may restructure the input from the environment. From this change in activity in the transaction, the worker may predict changes in either or both the coping behavior and environmental side. On the other hand, the independent variable activity may bring in additional resources and the dependent measure may be the changes in coping behaviors, and so forth. To state this another way, social work is more concerned with the consequence of action than the cause of action. It seems important that the profession continue to develop its perspective in a way that makes outcome measures more explicit. Social workers deal basically with three categories of coping behaviors and three categories of the impinging environment. These are not seen as mutually exclusive categories or as exhaustive. They seem to make clearer the areas in which social workers measure the effects of their intervention and to point out the breadth of practice phenomena.

Coping behavior. These three categories of coping behavior are: (1) coping behavior for surviving, (2) coping behavior for affiliating, and (3) coping behavior for growing and achieving. These categories help to set priorities. The first consideration is whether or not the client has the capacity to obtain and use the necessities for surviving; secondly, for affiliating. Both surviving and affiliating skills seem to be prerequisites to growing and achieving. Surviving, affiliating, growing, and achieving form a continuation of coping. Coping behaviors at any point in time are affected by information from past coping experience and build over time one on another.

Coping behaviors for surviving are those behaviors that enable the person to obtain and use resources that make it possible to continue life or activity. Such categories of surviving behaviors are the capacity to obtain food, shelter, clothing, and medical treatment; protection and locomotive skills.

Coping behaviors for affiliating are those behaviors that enable the person to unite in a close connection to others in the environment. Subcategories of affiliating behaviors are (1) the capacity to obtain and use personal relationships and (2) the ability to use organizations and organizational structures. Each individual is in contact with organized units such as family, school, clubs, and church.

Coping behaviors for growing and achieving are those behaviors that enable the person to perform for and to contribute to him or herself and others. Subcategories of coping behaviors for growing are developing and using (1) cognitive capacities, (2) physical capacities, (3) economic capacities, and (4) emotional capacities.

Environment. The environment can be seen as comprising (1) resources, (2) expectations, and (3) laws and policies. The categories of the environment do not have a priority of their own; rather, their priority gets established in the match with coping behaviors. That fact seems self-evident since the profession's major value is the person.

Resources are supplies that can be drawn on when needed or can be turned to for support or help as needed or, often, when desired. Pincus and Minahan have characterized resource systems as informal, formal, and societal. 10/ Informal resource systems consist of family, friends, neighbors, co-workers, and the like. Formal resource systems could be membership organizations or formal associations which promote the interest of members, such as Alcoholics Anonymous, Association for Retarded Children, and so forth. Societal resource systems are structured services and service institutions such as schools, hospitals, social security programs, courts, police agencies, and so forth. Resource systems may be adequate or inadequate and provide opportunities, incentives, or limitations. In many situations there are no resources to match the coping behaviors for surviving, affiliating, and growing.

Expectations are the patterned performance and normative obligations which are grounded in established societal structures. Expectations can involve roles and tasks. Social workers recognize these structures, but it is not their purpose as social workers to simply help people adapt to societal roles or to perform all expected tasks; although it is recognized that a positive role complementarity usually leads to greater mutual satisfaction and growth. Roles are the patterned, functional behaviors which are performed by a collection of persons. While these are normative patterns in the society, individuals do not always agree on the specific behaviors of a role. Roles do change since they are socially defined and functionally oriented. Sometimes this societal change is not acceptable to the individual and creates a mismatch between coping behaviors and the environment.

The concept of task is a way of describing the pressures placed on people by various life situations. These tasks "have to do with daily living, such as growing up in the family, and also with the common traumatic situations such as separation, illness, or financial difficulties." 11/ These tasks call for coping responses from the people involved in the situation.

Laws and policies are those binding customs or rules of conduct created by a controlling authority, such as legislation, legal decisions, and majority pressures. Subcategories are rights and responsibilities, procedures, sanctions, and inhibiting or restricting factors. As a category, laws and policies are seen as necessary and positive components of the environment. Yet it is also recognized that many single laws or policies have negative effects for groups of people. Some policies make survival more difficult, and in some cases--particularly for welfare clients--make affiliation almost impossible.

Expectations, laws, policies, and procedures are communicated through resources. The quality of output from a resource, such as a school, is very much affected by the state and national policies which have been adopted. The ultimate test of these policies is the match they make with coping behaviors of those persons with whom the school transacts, namely children. Thus, if these transactions are destructive to the coping behaviors of children, the policy is in need of change. Social workers are often in the best position for evaluating this match, whether it is in the procedures for implementing or in the policy.

TASKS IN SCHOOL SOCIAL WORK

While the school social work concentration has had a paucity of research, there have been at least three studies of "tasks" in school social work. The first of these was a study done by Lela Costin in the late 1960s, which addressed two questions: (1) How do practicing school social workers define the content of school social work and how do they give priorities to its parts? and (2) Do the tasks in school social work provide a basis for assigning responsibilities to staff with different kinds of training? 12/

Costin used a nationwide random sample of masters-degree social workers. A factor analysis of their responses to the importance of 107 items produced the following dimensions in order of priority: (1) casework services to child and parent; (2) caseload management; (3) interpreting school social work services; (4) clinical treatment of children with emotional problems; (5) liaison between the family and community agencies; (6) interpreting the child to the teacher; (7) educational counseling with the child and parents; and (8) leadership and policy change. From these data, Costin concluded that school social workers had conceptualized the major focus of their practice to be the individual child in relationship to his or her emotional problems and personal adjustment and that they had given much less importance to the role of professional leadership activities. She interpreted this finding as in keeping with the literature on school social work in the 1940s and 1950s. Costin further concluded that the main body of tasks as defined by school social workers did not lend themselves to assigning responsibilities to personnel with different levels of training.

A second study, by Alderson and Krishef in 1973, utilized Costin's formulation of task. 13/ It was conducted in the state of Florida, which has several disciplines and levels of training employed in school social work. At the time of this study, approximately 5 percent of the school social workers in Florida had MSW degrees. The data showed that there was a significant difference (at 0.05 level of confidence) on eight items. When the MSW social workers were compared to bachelor's-degree responses, there was a statistically significant difference on thirteen items. The overall findings in this study were very different from Costin's. The factors that were rated at the top in this study were (1) leadership and policymaking, (2) caseload management, (3) educational counseling with children and parents, and (4) interpreting school social work services. Also, the bottom factors were the same for all three groups: (4) interpreting the child to the teacher; (5) casework services to the child and his or her family; (6) liaison between the child and community agencies; and (7) clinical treatment of children with emotional problems. Alderson and Krishef suggest that this difference from Costin's study--particularly with leadership and policymaking, which are at opposite ends in these two studies--may be attributed to the models of social work appearing in the literature in the 1960s.

A third study of task, conducted by Meares in 1975, again utilized Costin's rating scale of task. 14/ Meares removed some items which had not proven useful in Costin's study, having a total of 84 items as compared to Costin's 107 items. Meares also used a random sample of school social workers drawn from a national roster. In this study, seven major dimensions of practice were found from the factor analysis of the data. In order of their importance these factors were (1) clarifying the child's problems with others, (2) preliminary tasks to the provision of social work services, (3) assessing the child's problems, (4) facilitating school-community pupil relationships, (5) educational counseling with the child and parents, (6) facilitating the utilization of community resources, and (7) leadership and policymaking.

While the differences between the Costin and Meares studies are not as great as those between the Costin and Alderson-Krishef studies, Meares also reached the conclusion that school social work is changing. The major focus has moved away from the primary emphasis on the individual child and his or her family in relationship to his or her personal problems, toward an emphasis on facilitating school-community-home relationships and providing educational counseling for the child and parents. Again Meares found, as Costin had, that leadership and policy change were rated low. In addition, Meares found that there was still some reluctance to deal with target groups rather than individuals.

In summary, there is evidence of movement in social work to a model dealing simultaneously with the student, the community, and the school. This kind of model is more in keeping with the central focus of social work, which is the interface between persons and their environment--an ecological perspective.

SOCIAL SERVICE MANPOWER: DIFFERENTIAL LEVELS

Social service manpower as used in the standards "refers to those engaged in aspects of social work practice, which involved helping activities that do not always require specific training or education but are intimately and necessarily related to professional social work and the accomplishment of social work objectives and services." 15/ The National Association of Social Workers (NASW) classification plan recognizes six levels of competence. From the six levels for all of social work practice, the four levels that are most useful for school social work are: (1) technician level, (2) social worker level, (3) graduate social worker level, and (4) certified social worker level.

In accord with the standards for social work manpower, the technician level is to be a part of a team or under the supervision of a graduate social worker. The professional social worker also functions under supervision. The graduate-level social worker is responsible for providing assistance to less advanced workers. After the graduate social worker acquires certification, she or he adds consultation responsibilities and interdisciplinary coordination to his or her potential responsibilities.

UTILIZING THE EXPANDED FRAMEWORK

Categories of outcome measures in social work have been conceptualized as: (1) coping behaviors for surviving, (2) coping behaviors for affiliating, (3) coping behaviors for growing and achieving, (4) resources, (5) expectations, and (6) laws and policies. 16/ These categories and the framework developed in this article will be utilized for establishing levels of practice in school social work: (1) the technician level may function at the level of matching surviving behaviors and resources at the basic level of practice, (2) the professional social worker will function at the level of matching facilitating behaviors and resources and expectations, (3) the graduate level of practice will function at the level of matching resources, expectations, with the growing and achieving behaviors, and laws and policies with all three levels of coping behaviors, and (4) the certified social worker would assume the graduate level functions, plus coordinating and supervising functions. As shown in Table 1, a taxonomy of functions for each level has been developed from this framework and a few suggested functions at each level are adopted from Costin-Meares studies on tasks in school social work.

The taxonomy is developed assuming a team approach, since only the graduate social worker functions autonomously. Levels I and II require supervision as does the Level III graduate social worker who wishes to obtain ACSW certification, which requires two years of supervision from a social worker who has certification. Also, it is assumed that a beginning graduate will not assume supervisory and coordinating responsibilities. Time is required for a new graduate to develop his or her level of functioning in the system. To utilize the taxonomy, a school social system would employ four team members, including a Level III who is obtaining his or her certification and a Level IV who is assuming coordinating and supervisory responsibilities.

Ratios. The following discussion of suggested ratios is developed from a base ratio of 1 worker to 1,000 students and assuming a middle-class socioeconomic level population and with little or no special services or populations. The ratio of 1 team to 4,000 assumes a team of 4: (1) technician level, (2) professional social worker level, (3) certified social worker level, and (4) a graduate-level social worker.

The ratio, developed for a single social worker functioning as an autonomous worker, requires a graduate social worker, preferably a certified social worker. This ratio assumes that the worker would function at all three levels of surviving, affiliating and growing. This would include crisis, remedial, and developmental services for children in the school system. When this level social worker is employed in the system where the ratio is 1 to 1,200 or more, it is usually necessary for her or him to perform only crisis and remedial and/or mandated services. Thus, it appears that the differential team approach is more economical. It is important, however, to recognize that the model presented here is based on projections, since these kinds of differential levels have had limited testing in the schools. The Alderson, Bedell, Goldstein, and Platt study of differential levels has been completed and does give some evidence of the usefulness of team approach. 17/

Teaming. The social work team is defined as "any grouping of social welfare personnel which has mutual responsibility for providing appropriate social services to a common clientele." 18/ The team is most often led by a certified social worker who must assume ultimate responsibility to make

(Text continues on page 148.)

Table 1. Taxonomy of Functions in School Social Work

Level I--Social Work Technician

Objectives

1. To match the surviving capacity of students with the existing resources in the environment.

2. To improve the basic quality of life for students.

3. To enhance basic skill development in individual children.

Functions (Examples)

1. Make referral to existing community resources and assist in their use.

2. Checks on attendance by making home visits in cases of prolonged or unexplained absences.

3. Obtains from parents information about the family's functioning (financial and employment situation; satisfaction or discord in family relationships).

4. Acts as a liaison between a family and a social agency to insure that, following referral, service gets under way (by interpreting the lifestyle of a family to agency worker and, in turn, the agency requirements and expectations to the family).

5. Encourages children and families to ask for and make maximum use of community "supplementary" or "enabling" services (day care, homemaker, summer camps, Y's, parent education groups, various home helps).

Level II--Professional Social Work (BSW)

Objectives

1. To develop affiliating behavior in the child through direct work individually or in groups or through changing the resource and expectations to the child.

Functions (Examples)

1. Direct services to children identified or referred as culturally and educationally disadvantaged, attendance problems, predelinquent, and as victims of suspected child abuse and neglect.

2. Consults with other special service personnel to develop and coordinate an overall treatment approach for the child.

3. Working with severely disturbed, utilizing classroom management skills and groups of parents re: home management as it ties with teacher instruction.

4. Participate in research projects.

Table 1. Taxonomy of Functions in School Social Work (continued)

Level III & IV--Graduate and Certified Social Worker

Objectives

1. To enhance the growth potential of children through group activities.

2. To intervene in the school system in ways that change the expectations for the child.

3. To contribute to knowledge in school social work through research and publications.

4. To enhance school and community relationships.

5. To develop new resource programs for children.

6. To evaluate policy and formulate new policy and procedures in the school system.

Functions (Examples)

1. In-service training of teachers with respect to group dynamics as applied to classroom management skills.

2. Set up, develop the mechanics for, and conduct parent groups composed of persons with similar concerns.

3. Help interpret to the community the school administrative policies which have to do with pupil welfare.

4. Provide administrators with the knowledge to develop cooperative working relationships with community agencies.

5. Participate in and develop research. Publish new findings and perspectives on social work services in the school setting.

6. Help bring about change in the system of school-community-pupil relations which will alleviate stress upon groups of pupils.

7. Help to bring about new outside-of-school programs through work with other individuals and community groups (recreation, day care, health clinics, drug abuse).

8. Assist in the recruitment of social work personnel.

Level IV--Certified ACSW Social Worker (See also Level III)

Objectives

1. Assist in the education and training of social work personnel (other team members and field instruction of graduate social workers).

Functions

1. Coordinator of social work teams.

2. Coordinator of interdisciplinary team.

3. Supervisor of Level I, II, and III social workers.

assignments of activities to each team member. The number and kinds of positions on any particular team is an idiosyncratic matter, related to the number of variables included in the situation being handled. The team which has been suggested here is a four-member team. The team positions in the model presented here are taken from the NASW manpower guidelines.

In many team situations, the relationship between team members is a purely collaborative one. That is not the case in the team described here. There is also a hierarchical relationship between members of the team. There is, however, room for collaborative activities with respect to individual case situations, as well as group projects and program activities. These collaborative activities would be encouraged.

A Preferred Team Structure. Perhaps a more ideal team model would be to have two Level II workers, one Level III, and one Level IV worker. This model would allow for much greater autonomy for each worker. The Level I task could be included with the Level II task. Because of the more advanced functioning, the Level IV worker would be freer of some supervisory responsibilities and could develop more collaborative functions between workers. This is probably the only structure that would allow for developing all three levels of functioning completely, including preventive activities. Suggested ratios for these combinations are as follows:

(1) Two Level II workers; one Level III worker and one Level IV worker - ratio $\frac{1\ team}{4,500}$ (assuming middle-class, social-economic conditions with little or no special services).

Three Level II workers; one Level IV worker - ratio $\frac{1\ team}{4,200}$

There are some additional variables that might influence the ratio of school social workers to school populations. For example, such community characteristics as socioeconomic level, resource network, delinquency rates, and so forth need to be considered. In addition, certain characteristics of the school--such as incidences of dropouts, availability of other pupil personnel services, student turnover, bilingual population, special classes, and chemical abuse cases--also need consideration. All variables in the school system and its environment as well as the service network are important considerations in determining ratios. Also, the number of buildings involved will affect the ratio. For example, it is possible to work with a larger number of students under the same building administration. In addition, the large number of mandated functions, as a result of federal legislation, has increased the number of social workers in the schools, but at the same time has added additional time-consuming responsibilities.

Some examples of ratios with a fully trained single worker in the school with special conditions, and offering service at all levels are as follows: (1) total school with no poverty conditions, and no special education concentration or minority population--ratio of 1 to 1,200, (2) same population but only crisis and remedial and consultation services--ratio of 1 to 1,500, (3) same population but only major crisis and some consultation services--ratio of 1 to 2,000, (4) total school plus a small special education concentration, ratio of 1 to 1,000, (5) total school plus a special education and poverty concentration--ratio of 1 to 750, (6) special program assignments, for example, a prekindergarten program or a hearing-impaired program or a preschool retard program--ratio of 1 to 200.

It is not possible to cover all the variables or combinations of variables that may exist in the school and affect worker-student ratio. The above examples are offered as suggested guidelines to be considered in planning for social work personnel.

SUMMARY

This article describes a broad social work practice model with particular application to school social work. Various school social studies of task in school social work have been presented. From this broad practice framework, a taxonomy of levels of practice in the school and suggested ratios of workers to school population has been developed. Attention has been given to the possible task functions at each level.

NOTES AND REFERENCES

1. William E. Gordon, "Basic Constructs for an Integrative and Generative Conception of Social Work," in General Systems Approach: Contributions Toward a Holistic Conception of Social Work (New York: Council on Social Work Education, 1969), pp. 5-11; Harriett Bartlett, "Seeking the Strengths of Social Work," in Common Base of Social Work Practice (New York: National Association of Social Workers, 1970), pp. 13-20; Will Schwartz, "Private Troubles and Public Issues: One Social Work Job or Two?" in Social Welfare Forum (New York: Columbia University Press, 1969), pp. 22-43; Gordon Hearn, ed., The General Systems Approach: Contributions Toward an Holistic Conception of Social Work (New York: Council on Social Work Education, 1969), p. 65; Robert W. Belmont and Robert M. Ryan, The Practice of Social Work (2nd ed.; Belmont, Calif.: Wadsworth Publishing Co., 1974), p. 360; Allen Pincus and Anne Minahan, Social Work Practice: Model and Method (Itasca, Ill.: F.E. Peacock Publishers, 1973), p. 3; Beulah R. Compton and Burt Galaway, Social Work Processes (Homewood, Ill.: Dorsey Press, 1975), p. 70; Alex Gitterman and Carel Germain, "Social Work Practice: A Life Model," Social Service Review, 50 (December 1976), pp. 601-610; Marjorie McQueen Monkman, "A Framework for Effective Social Work Intervention in the Public Schools," School Social Work Journal, 1 (Fall 1976), Monkman, "A Broader, More Comprehensive View of School Social Work Practice," School Social Work Journal, 2 (Spring 1978); and Carol Meyer, Ralph Garber and Constance W. Williams, Specialization in the Social Work Profession (New York: Council on Social Work Education, Commission on Educational Planning, Subcommittee on Specialization, 1979).

2. Gordon, op. cit., pp. 5-11.

3. Ibid.

4. Ibid., p. 8.

5. Ibid.

6. Ibid., p. 9.

7. Ibid., p. 11.

8. Carel B. Germain and Alex Gitterman, The Life Model of Social Work Practice (New York: Columbia University Press, 1980), pp. 4-5.

9. For another and more complete use of the expanded framework, see Marjorie McQueen Monkman, "The Contribution of the Social Worker to the Public Schools" in Robert Constable, ed., A Federal Mandate for School Social Work Services: Meeting the Challenge. (New York: Haworth Press, 1981).

10. Pincus and Minahan, op. cit., p. 108.

11. Bartlett, op. cit., p. 96.

12. Lela B. Costin, "An Analysis of the Tasks in School Social Work," Social Service Review, 43 (September 1969), pp. 274-285.

13. John J. Alderson and Curtis H. Krishef, "Another Perspective on Tasks in School Social Work," Social Casework, 54 (December 1973), pp. 591-600.

14. Paula Allen Meares, "Analysis of Tasks in School Social Work," Social Work, 22 (May 1977), pp. 196-201.

15. NASW Standards for Social Work Services in Schools, NASW Policy Statement No. 7 (Washington, D.C.: National Association of Social Workers, 1978).

16. For a more complete discussion of differential levels and ratios, see Marjorie M. Monkman, "The Specialization of School Social Work and a Model for Differential Levels of Practice" in Dean G. Miller, ed., Differential Levels of Student Support Services: Including Crisis Remedial and Preventive/Developmental Approaches, to be published by Minnesota Department of Education, St. Paul.

17. John J. Alderson, Rebecca Bedell, Harris Goldstein, and Judith Platt, "Evaluation and Differential Use of Staff: A Model," Social Work in Education, 2 (July 1980), pp. 40-54.

18. Thomas L. Briggs, "An Overview of Social Work Teams," in Donald Brieland, Thomas Briggs, and Paul Leuenberger, eds., The Team Model of Social Work Practice (Syracuse, N.Y.: Syracuse University School of Social Work, 1973), p. 4.

NOTES